PROFESSIONAL ENGINEERING PRACTICE ETHICAL ASPECTS

Carson Morrison, P. Eng.
Professor Emeritus
Civil Engineering
University of Toronto

Philip Hughes, P. Eng.
Professor Emeritus
Mechanical Engineering
University of Toronto

McGRAW-HILL RYERSON LIMITED
Toronto   Montréal   New York   St. Louis
San Francisco   Auckland   Bogotá   Guatemala
Hamburg   Johannesburg   Lisbon   London   Madrid
Mexico   New Delhi   Panama   Paris   San Juan
São Paulo   Singapore   Sydney   Tokyo

REVISED EDITION

ISBN 0-07-548834-5

Printed and bound in Canada by John Deyell Company

1 2 3 4 5 6 7 8 9 0   D   1 0 9 8 7 6 5 4

Care has been taken to trace ownership of copyright material contained
in this text. The publishers will gladly take any information that will
enable them to rectify any reference or credit in subsequent editions.

Canadian Cataloguing in Publication Data

Morrison, Carson, date
   Professional engineering practice

Includes bibliographical references.
ISBN 0-07-548834-5

1. Engineering ethics.   I. Hughes, Philip.   II. Title.

TA157.M67 1984   174'.962   C84-098495-2

TABLE OF CONTENTS

CONTRIBUTORS

Oswald Hall,, Ph.D.
Professor Emeritus in Sociology
University of Toronto
Chapter 2

Howard Bexon, P.Eng.,
Manager, Product Development Engineering
Transportation Products, Dofasco Inc.
Chapter 6

Hugh Adcock, P.Eng.
Assistant Deputy Minister (Retired)
Ontario Ministry of Transportation and Communications
Chapter 5

John Kean, P.Eng.
President, Canadian Standards Association
Chapter 7

John Stevens, P.Eng.
Manager, Engineering Product Concepts
Atomic Energy of Canada Limited
Chapter 8 and a case study in Chapter 11

PREFACE

Throughout this book, the word "man" is used in the generic sense. Whenever appropriate in the context the singular is intended to include the plural and the masculine to include the feminine.

In the province of Ontario the Professional Engineers Act (the Act) defines "professional engineer" and the "practice of professional engineering." The Act limits the right to practise professional engineering to persons with qualifications set out in the Act. Among these qualifications (except for "any person performing his duties with the Canadian Armed Forces") is membership in the Association of Professional Engineers of Ontario (APEO) or the holding of a licence to practise issued by the APEO.

The APEO is bound to accept as a member any person meeting the above and the further required qualifications (residence, age, engineering education, experience, good character), and willing to subscribe to and follow "a code of ethics containing standards of conduct designed for the protection of the public . . . in the practice of engineering." This Code of Ethics is to be (and now has long been) prepared and published by the APEO, and the processes of recourse by the APEO against any member or licensee who is at fault with respect to the Code of Ethics are stipulated in the Act.

Essentially, the engineering profession in Ontario—and this is so in all of the other provinces in Canada, with some variations in details and mechanisms—is self-regulating under the Act and, along with certain by-laws and regulations intended to assure orderly and systematic conduct in relations between the profession and the public, the Code of Ethics is the basic document by which the practice of the individual is governed.

The objective of this book is to enhance the understanding of applicants for membership in APEO—and, with respect, in the associations in other Canadian jurisdictions, each of which has comparable duties and authority—of the ethical obligations the members undertake. Many candidates have not been accustomed to this aspect of engineering because in a preponderantly technical education most of the problem-solving relies on interpretation of "hard" knowledge, facts or calculable probabilities and risks. As a general rule, candidates have not often had to deal with the interpretation of rights, privileges and obligations, of relations between professionals, of the language of the Act, Regulations, By-Laws and Code of Ethics. Against this perception of what has hampered some candidates in previous examinations in the subject, this book has been prepared.

Some of the material offered has been adapted from that presented for several years by lecturers in the course in Professional Practice—Ethics, in the School of Continuing Studies and now in the Continuing Education Program in the Faculty of Applied Science and Engineering, University of Toronto; the authors express their appreciation and gratitude to these lecturers for permission to use this material. Names of the topics and the lecturers and their affiliations are given in the List of Contributors.

To assist it in making a dependable determination of the qualifications of each candidate for admission to APEO, particularly with respect to the ethical considerations in engineering education, the Association in 1981 inaugurated a two-part Admission Examination. Part A of that examination is in Professional Practice and Ethics, the subject of this book.

The authors acknowledge the kind permission of:
1) APEO to use text from its Manual of Professional Practice;
2) The Institute of Public Administration of Canada, to use excerpts from its Ethical Guidelines for Government Employees by Kenneth Kernaghan;
3) The Royal Bank of Canada, to use the Royal Bank Letter, Vol. 62, No. 1 Jan/Feb 1981.

ADDENDUM TO THE PREFACE

Originally the material in this book was compiled and presented as a text for candidates who were preparing for the examination 'Professional Engineering Practice: Ethics', one of the requirements for admission to the Association of Professional Engineers of the Province of Ontario. Because ethics is an essential of professional practice the Code of Ethics of the Association was used as the principal guideline to the subject.

There are twelve professional engineering jurisdictions in the provinces and territories of Canada; each has its own Code or Canons of Ethics. An overall similarity and harmony of intent pervades these codes, yet sufficient difference in emphasis arises in wording and arrangement to warrant the inclusion of all twelve codes in the second printing. Not only may it make the book more widely appropriate but for Ontario candidates it illustrates and emphasizes that they share a common heritage of ethical principles (as they do of education and training) with professional engineers in other jurisdictions.

CHAPTER 1

DEFINITIONS

A clear understanding of the meanings of the key words relevant to the subject is essential to an understanding of the ethical aspects of professional engineering practice. For that reason, this chapter lists, defines and comments on the meanings, origins and usage of some of these words.

Definitions are selected from the Oxford Universal Dictionary, third edition, 1955; several quotations are taken from Fowler's *A Dictionary of Modern English Usage* (second edition, 1965). Definitions and quotations represent points of anchorage upon which the authors have hung a discursive context.

An early recognition of the professional engineer appears in Adam Smith's *The Wealth of Nations*, 1776, where in pursuing the subject of the division of labour, the author speaks of

> . . . those who are called philosophers, or men of specula-
> tion, whose trade it is not to do any thing, but to observe
> every thing, and who, upon that account, are often capable
> of combining together the powers of the most distant and
> dissimilar objects.

It is doubtful that this quaint discription could be improved two centuries later; if we try to render it in modern and precise terms we encounter the same difficulty as when we try rewriting familiar Biblical passages in today's idiom with the hope that a clearer understanding may be effected: too often the pith of the original is lost, and the meaning may be limited in scope by the very precision we have attempted.

We might complain of Adam Smith's job description, ''whose trade it is not to do any thing'', on the grounds that the professional engineer today is likely to be run off his feet with duties,

1

until we recall that Adam Smith's contemporaries—the giant Watt and the formidable characters whose bridges, canals and harbour works foreshadowed and patterned our accomplishments—were half craftsmen, half philosophers, and that they exhibited enormous capacity for work in their lifetimes. But they did not produce goods for commerce. Their accomplishments loom to this day and remain our pride and our envy, but were not the "doing of things" in Adam Smith's context of the division of labour.

ENGINE; ENGINEER

The dictionary tells us that the word "engine" is derived from the Latin "ingenium" (and thus obviously related to ingenious and, a connection less obvious but interesting, to engender or beget). The word is given a series of meanings. It was in use before the steam engine; its original meaning was "an instance or product of ingenuity." Likewise, the word "engineer" preceded the steam engine, and in its early use was attached to one who contrives, designs or invents; an inventor, a plotter. We now confine "engine" to the engine as we know it and other meanings are seldom encountered. "Engineer," however, when we couple to it the adjective "professional," has retained its original meaning of one who contrives, designs, etcetera, because the professional engineer is by no means always associated with the engine.

THE OPERATOR ENGINEER

To-day, those most intimately concerned with the engine are stationary, railway, and other operating engineers, who do not formally share a duty that could be described as ". . . not to do any thing, but to observe every thing," and to whom we deny the designation professional, which we have arrogated to ourselves. Observe every thing they may not, but observe their engines they certainly do, and if our philosopher or man of speculation has added wisdom to his faculties, he will seek the benefit of the observations of these half-brothers, and accord them proper respect. Indeed, if our philosopher has occasion to cling to a walkway rail in the engine room of a ship in a heavy sea, or to watch the flight engineer vigilant before the array of instruments that monitor the great engines that are shouting the glory of God at fifty thousand pounds thrust, the sense of respect will be strong in him.

PROFESS; PROFESSION; VOCATION

In its widest sense, "to profess" is to declare openly, to affirm before the world some loyalty, belief, adherence to a school of thought, or to claim openly the command of some field of knowledge. That field of knowledge is the profession. A narrower meaning of the word is that of the calling or vocation by which a livelihood is earned, without, at least in its use in the past, a particular connotation of learning. Our dictionary gives us an example of usage: "Joseph, her Spouse, by Profession a carpenter." This seems to suggest English usage early in the seventeenth century.

THE "LEARNED PROFESSIONS"

Common today is a definition of "profession": a vocation in which a professed knowledge of some department of learning is used in its application to the affairs of others, or in the practice of an art founded upon it.

A somewhat different, but not conflicting, definition of "profession" comes from Webster's *New World Dictionary* (Second College Edition, 1970): a vocation or occupation requiring advanced education and training and involving intellectual skills, as medicine, law, theology, engineering, teaching, etcetera.

From before the Industrial Revolution, say about 1700, to the late years of the nineteenth century we spoke of three learned professions—divinity, law and medicine—and of two not associated with learning—the military profession and the profession of gentleman (!). These thrived or starved as the case might be for the individual; all five enjoyed an irreproachable respectability in the middle class of society.

TODAY'S PROFESSIONAL

Gone is the public consensus that so limited the professions. We seldom use the tag "learned" now, but to apply to a calling the designation "profession" we tend to require that there be a "professed knowledge of some department of learning" to justify it.   3

This, used as a criterion, gives us no direction as to what is to be considered acceptable as a department of learning; as with the mathematical model that shows what critical decision has to be made, it leaves the rest to us. In fact, except as we are members of the public, we do not make any rule or decision in the matter, for it is public repute, the public image, that decides whether a calling is a profession in the eyes of the world.

DO WE CARE?

Yes, we do care. We believe the learning we profess and apply is beyond question adequate, and we believe the engineering profession has been accepted by the public for many years now. But our caring goes deeper than concern with public regard, goes into other and more subtle aspects of professionalism, into the satisfaction and happiness each of us, as an individual, derives from his practice.

For years, texts on management have given us lists of human satisfactions for which provision should be made in planning industrial working conditions. But for the individual practitioner of the beneficent and terrible art we profess, let us look beyond the relatively obvious range of the working place. In every man and woman there is a flicker of desire, most of the time subconscious, to serve some end quite beyond personal welfare, beyond the need to be admired, to be loved, to be procreator of future generations. Indeed, this may be the presence of the abstract: love. And happy, if seldom prosperous, are the few in whose lives this is the dynamic, who might say, as the father of the famous Mayo brothers is said to have said, "There is no greater disgrace than to die rich."

We number few saints among us. But as we achieve command of the "department of learning" that is the province of engineering, that faint flame may reveal a further knowledge: that by venturing into this profession, we have pledged ourselves, perhaps inadvertently, not only to public safety as it is affected by our works, but to grave concern with the quality of the future of our kind. And if your authors have adverted to imaginative language in expressing these solemn thoughts, it is an attempt to crack the shell of superficiality in which the meaning of the word "professionalism" is so often encased, an attempt to capture something of the notion of ordainment that is implicit in the term; it is a summons to "think big" about what we do.

4

ETHICS AND MORALITY

These words are both defined and differentiated in one golden sentence given us by Fowler: "Ethics is the science of morals and morals are the practice of ethics."

Let us put Fowler's sentence in a slightly more explanatory cast: Ethics is the science by which people draw up sets of moral imperatives; the morals of an individual are the way in which he or she applies such a set of imperatives in his or her actions.

Note that the word "ethics," written and spoken with the final *s*, is a singular noun. A prevailing code of morality is one of the meanings given in the dictionary, and is the closest to what we generally intend by the word.

We encounter no less than twenty-three square inches of small print in the defining of "moral" as a noun, adjective and even verb (rare), with "morals" as the plural noun. From this vast array we boldly extract for "morals": "character or disposition; distinction between right and wrong, or good and evil, in relation to action."

The word "ethic," without the final *s*, is properly used as an adjective, and is synonymous with the word "ethical." As a noun, it means ethics; it is not properly used to refer to one canon of a group, or set, of canons. For instance, the Protestant ethic, sometimes cited in management texts, refers to the code of ethics of Protestantism, not to a particular part of such a code.

Sometimes the negative, or converse, forms of words have peculiar shades of meaning. Fowler says that since the word "immoral" is popularly associated with sexual immorality, the word "unethical" has come into vogue as an adjective that describes the person who is immoral in other ways, especially in violating the accepted code of a profession or business. The words "right" and "wrong" and "good" and "wicked" seem now to be old-fashioned.

A previous mention of the twenty-three square inches of small print used to define a single word was intended to convey an idea of your authors' diligence; applying it they have concluded that the usage adopted by the Engineers' Council for Professional Development (ECPD) is, as might be expected, rigorous. ECPD speaks of its "revised set of Canons of Ethics (1973)." A code of ethics is a set of canons. We can speak of a certain canon in a code without having to use words like "rule" or "precept," neither of which has quite the same meaning as canon.

Associated historically with ethics is Hippocrates of Alexandria, third century BC, whose writings about medicine are said to deal explicitly with ethical aspects of that art—too explicitly for modern practice, perhaps, for the Hippocratic Oath (see under "Medicine—History of" in the Encyclopaedia Brittanica, 1946, volume 15), tacitly or openly avowed by medical practitioners for many centuries, has been abandoned in some parts of the world in recent years.

CODES OF ETHICS, WRITTEN AND UNWRITTEN

In all walks of life, codes of ethics appear, drawn up to express the "character or disposition in relation to action" of a group of persons of common vocation or interest. The extent to which the code is observed by the members of the group, and probably the extent to which it is taken seriously by the public, are both subject to much the same variables: apart from the strong factors of tradition and recognition of the trade, profession or common interest as an entity in the life of the community, an obvious factor is the authority of the group vis-à-vis its members. In a self-regulating profession like ours, a member can be struck from the professional register in cases of grossly unethical conduct, but many groups, although the members subscribe to a code, have only the withdrawal of esteem or companionship, or of a reserved title with which to enforce it. An interesting and almost converse case is that of business groups, often loosely knit, which, having no code in writing, yet wield a very real power to enforce compliance with one or more moral principles. In commerce and finance, contracts that often involve huge sums of money are made by word of mouth. That prime canon, that a man's word shall be as good as his bond, obtains without question. And the enforcement is absolute: to transgress this single canon is to be excluded from high trading circles without forgiveness this side of the grave. Remembering this helps us avoid complacency when we contemplate the written code we subscribe to in our chosen profession.

STATUS; ESTEEM; IMAGE

We are frequently reminded of our status as members of the engineering profession, and we are expected to behave in a manner appropriate to that status. The word "status" is defined as "legal standing as determined by membership of some class of persons or things enjoying certain rights or subject to certain limitations.'' Let us dismiss *things* by citing an example given in the dictionary, the status of enemy merchant vessels, and consider *persons*. Our own status is that common to all citizens, except that we enjoy the certain additional rights (in Ontario) conferred upon us by the Professional Engineers Act. That is, we have a particular status that is assumed by the individual upon registration. It is clearly defined; we hold it under the law so long as our name stands on the register.

Status, of itself, implies nothing about public regard. A tinker doing thirty days for being drunk and disorderly has a status, just as does an archbishop; the tinker is subject to certain limitations while the archbishop enjoys certain rights, but the condition of each fits the definition of status. The esteem, however, in which each status is held is very different.

The word ''esteem'' has several definitions, such as ''to evaluate,'' as a verb, or ''valuation,'' as a noun, the noun being further described as favourable opinion, regard, respect, which is the meaning we intend here.

Persons who hold a recognizable status, which they themselves esteem, tend to constrain themselves to act their part in the world so as to communicate that esteem to others. It is a human trait, a natural desire. Further, such persons, jealous of the esteem they cultivate in others, will resent a fellow member of the group who will not be subject to the same constraints, holding such person to be one who destroys what they strive to build. In such a sequence, the idea of a common image possesses the group, and often, as our own Association has done in the past, the group discusses and publishes among its members various ways for achieving it.

With some care we have differentiated *status* and *esteem*, the first susceptible to measurement and the second not, but no less important. We have come to, and already employed, the word ''image''; we all know how it is used, perhaps overused, today. The dictionary emphasizes the element of artificiality, not only by giving us the Latin root, which is common with that of the verb ''to imitate,'' but in the definition itself.

''Image'' is the artificial representation of a person; a mental picture or impression; an idea, conception. We cannot depend upon nature; each of us must design his image to be the picture he wants to appear in the minds of others.

Most of the discussions on the subject published among our   7 own members had to do with participation in public affairs, activity in good causes, with being good citizens, and so on. The thesis addressed was the entirely rational one that popularity can, and should, enhance esteem. But there was no direct aim at the particular rights of our status as affecting the design of the image we were to seek to project. Our Code of Ethics, is, of course, directly concerned with our behaviour in the practice reserved to us, and gives full attention to the public to the extent that our works affect it. But the Code does not normally reach the public, and if it did, it is somewhat remote from the opinion-forming contacts that create the public image of the group.

Perhaps, for each one of us, it boils down to our minimizing the artificiality by being, and being seen to be, trustworthy in all matters outside our practice, just as we are trustworthy, and are seen to be trustworthy, in working relations with our fellow engineers. The good-citizenship aspects we can design to suit our capabilities and desires.

CHAPTER 2

THE PROFESSIONS IN PRESENT-DAY SOCIETY

In present-day society professions are very numerous. This was not always the case. Historically the professions were three: medicine, law and the priesthood. Professionals looked after one's health, one's fortune, and one's soul.

In each case they dealt with a fearfully consequential set of affairs. One's health is continually threatened by unknown dangers. One's affairs are at the mercy of the law, which seems infinitely mysterious. The fate of one's soul has been a source of endless anxiety. The three great historic professions attended to the central problems of the human animal.

Because they dealt with matters of transcending importance, these professions have been accorded a great deal of autonomy and freedom to go about their work. Historically their advice, and their orders, were unquestioned. They have been called the "free independent" professions, because they were free from control by any other part of society. It is small wonder that they have been admired and envied by other occupations, or that other occupations have tried to copy them. In all societies they have ranked at the top of the social order as far as income and prestige are concerned. Most occupations that aspire to be professions tend to model themselves on the historical professions.

In present-day society one can count the professions by the score. The later ones do not seem to provide such important services as did the three mentioned earlier. Dentistry is a fairly recent profession, and it provides a distinctive service. But dentistry is not a life-and-death sort of enterprise. However, it does seem that in the course of time new professions do arise, generally because society comes to accept their services as important.

In our day the condition of our teeth, and the accompanying smile, seem almost as important as the condition of our souls.

On the other hand, many of the newer professions do not provide a service to the individual person. They provide services for organizations. In our society, organizations have an importance comparable to that of persons. In a very real sense one can say that there are professions that look after the health of organizations (here accountants come to mind); there are others that look after their fortunes (economists, for one); and if the organization has a ''soul'' the public-relations specialist attends to its welfare.

SCIENCE AND THE PROFESSIONS: THE CASE OF ENGINEERING

If we consider engineering as a profession it is clear that the ''services'' are rarely provided for a person. Bridges are built for railways, skyscrapers are built for companies, oil wells are drilled for corporations, mines are dug for business concerns, and so the list goes on. In modern societies the services performed for organizations rank in importance with those provided for individual persons.

Nonetheless, engineering shares many of the earmarks of the historic professions, among which one stands out as deserving special consideration. This is the relation to science. Sociologists argue as to which is more consequential for modern society, the work of the scientist or that of the professions. Clearly each has transformed the nature of work. Clearly the two developments are interwoven in an intricate way. Their fortunes and their futures are intertwined.

On the other hand, in any particular profession, they are rarely in step. Sometimes science outruns technology, and sometimes technology leads science. In mechanical engineering the steam engine was widely used long before scientists understood the principles involved in the field of energy. By contrast in electrical engineering the nature of electricity was discovered long before anyone contrived any use for it.

One of the lively aspects of any profession is the way it deals with the growth of scientific knowledge. If it ignores science, as the priesthood has done in various times and places, a profession may decline or even disappear. At the other extreme, if a profession tries to use the full resources of science it may have great difficulty handling practical problems. One thinks of the painful condition of the engineers who seek ways to deal with nuclear wastes, and with the responsibilities of atomic explosions. Such engineers may be looked on as the "enemies" of society, rather than the providers of important professional services.

While the problem seems distinctive when stated as above, one can see that we have here a very general feature of all professions. It is the matter of the relation of the profession to the body of scientific knowledge. For any profession we can ask the following questions:

Does the profession make use of a substantial body of scientific knowledge, or a slender body?

Does the profession have procedures that keep its practising members abreast of the changes in scientific knowledge?

Are the members of the profession themselves involved in research, that is, in the actual creation of new knowledge, or does it relinquish this task to others?

Are the members of the profession on the forefront of the research enterprise, or are they content with modest efforts in this respect?

These four questions are, in a sense, measures of the welfare of any profession. The members of each profession need to look at them, fairly and squarely, as a guide to understanding where they are heading.

THE SOCIAL CONTROL OF THE PROFESSIONS

As noted, the professions have striven to become "free and independent." At one level this has meant being "free" to charge substantial fees for their services, and hence to become financially independent. But in a more important way "free and independent" meant the right to decide what should be done for a client and how it should be done. In essence this means that the professional decides what is right for the client to do. In effect the professional assures society that the client is being advised in the most appropriate way. Wherever this occurs the professional becomes the final arbiter of what is good for society. Without doubt this is a tremendous privilege that is granted to the profes-

11

sion. The other side of the coin is the awesome responsibility it involves. Hence one can say that the professions in society enjoy very high prestige insofar as they have been granted privileges of this order and have shouldered the responsibilities that go with them.

Generally, professionals are a bit more eager to have the privileges of their way of life than they are to accept the responsibilities. On the other hand society is more prone to limit the privileges and to insist that professionals live up to their responsibilities. Hence there is a continuous tension between the professions and the larger society, and a continuous effort by society to limit the autonomy of professions.

This tension arises for two reasons. On the one hand more and more persons in our society are expecting and demanding more and better services from the professions. They are demanding more from the professions in terms of the quantity and quality of their services. At the same time organizations are expecting more from their professionals, and laying more responsibilities on them. This is so because professional failures have terrible consequences for organizations. If a dam bursts or a plane crashes, if a bridge collapses or a factory explodes or a fire-protection system fails, the effects are felt not by one individual person, but by possibly a multitude of persons. Hence society continually seeks new ways to ensure that professionals live up to responsibilities, and these responsibilities themselves become ever more inclusive and more detailed.

The efforts to control professions run along three distinct paths. The first path is to create a legal code. In this case the state, or some branch of government, establishes rules governing the particular profession. It does this by legislation, by an act of the legislature that sets out in legal terms what are the responsibilities and privileges, the rights and the duties, of the members of the profession. Such an act requires that there be a set of inspectors who regularly inspect the ongoing work of the professionals, to assure that the quality and quantity of their work is adequate. Besides these, there are legal penalties set forth and applied to those professionals whose work is insufficient in the eyes of the inspectors. Altogether these represent a system that assures society that professional services can be trusted.

The second path to social control is reflected in a code of ethics. In this case the procedures for control are vested with the profession itself, that is, the profession viewed as a collectivity.

In this case the members of a profession set up some sort of association, which in its own right establishes the rules and regulations under which its members work. Such an association may establish the scale of fees and the responsibilities of its members. It may also set up machinery to check the work of its members, and ways to punish those who fail to adhere to the code of ethics. But those who do this are members of the profession, and not the police and the judges of the larger society. To say that a profession has professional autonomy means that it handles the matters just discussed.

The third form of social control can be described as a code of honour. This is not a written document like a legal code or a code of ethics. Rather it is something internal, as is the case with one's conscience. In many professions one finds a more highly developed sense of professional honour, which guides members in what they should and should not do. A code of honour works without any need of inspectors, or of police to enforce it. Such a code may demand higher standards of people than colleagues would expect. Yet it may be a source of deep professional pride to be able to live up to a code of honour.

These are the three basic forms of social control. The first is exercised by an agency outside of the profession. The second is made effective by the collective efforts of all the members of the profession. The third operates within the individual member of the profession, even though it has been learned from other colleagues. It would seem that, in order for the members of a profession to live up to their responsibilities, one or more of the three codes mentioned must be functioning.

PROFESSIONAL ASSOCIATIONS

Almost all the professions have established one or more associations, which take care of the collective interests of the profession. Some professions have one association that handles many functions, while others have a variety of associations that are more specialized. It should be noted that there is usually one compulsory association whereas the others tend to be voluntary.

The medical profession has a very elaborate set of associations. Over the past century six very different types have emerged. One is called a "College," and it is compulsory that all physicians join it. This one is established by law. It controls the licensing of the members, and is responsible for their registra-

13

tion. It has substantial responsibilities for education and for the examination of candidates. Another of its main functions is the formulation of a code of ethics and its enforcement.

A second association is largely economic in character. It sets the fee schedule for the members, and bargains with the government regarding charges therein. In effect it is the political arm of the profession. Unlike the College it is a voluntary association, though almost all members belong to it as well as to the College.

There is a third association that caters to professional self-improvement, and also opportunities for sociability for the members. In it members come together to listen to lectures and join in discussion. This association has both a library and a museum that contribute to the intellectual life of the profession. They help the members to stay abreast of developments in the field of science.

Along with these three there is another that concentrates on the concerns of the women members of the profession, while a fifth looks after the special interests of students and the doctors just starting on their careers, the interns.

Finally, there are smaller associations made up of the doctors who are associated with a specific hospital. They come together to handle the various problems that arise in the daily working of a modern hospital, particularly as these problems bear on the welfare and working conditions of doctors.

It should be noted that each of these various forms of association handles a very consequential part of the affairs of the medical profession. As noted above some professions manage to survive with only one association. In those cases, of course, the tasks are all placed on the shoulders of one executive group. In general, the more highly developed a profession becomes the more specialized association will it develop.

To an increasing degree, the welfare of any profession is borne by the associations it develops. The officers of the association carry very consequential responsibilities. Their tasks require much time, energy and imagination. It is a continuing but inescapable task to select the gifted members to fill these positions. It is equally important that the officers reflect the long-term interests as well as the wishes of the members of the profession. These matters are part of the larger social problem of making democracy work.

CHAPTER 3

REGULATION OF THE PROFESSION

The province of Ontario and other jurisdictions are responsible for the regulation of engineers and other professionals. In Ontario, the Professional Engineers Act was enacted in 1922. Several amendments have been made since that time to recognize relevant changes that have occurred; the most recent amendment was in 1972.

Jargon is a phraseology peculiar to a particular class, profession or trade, for example the jargon of the law, or "legalese." Because so much of the wording of the Act is legalese, the authors present here the following comments on some of the words and expressions relevant to the regulation of the engineering profession.

Academy, association, college, council, institute, institution, order, society (licensing and non-licensing): all these titles, and others, are used to designate what is described by one of the definitions of "college" as: "an organized society of persons performing certain common functions and possessing special rights and privileges," a meaning in which there is, of course, no connotation of desks and blackboards.

Where the "common functions" are the practice of a profession or the following of an occupation, where the "special" rights and privileges are related to these functions, and where the "organized society" determines the qualifications for its membership, we have a profession or occupation that is in some measure self-regulating. The POC Report discussed later in this chapter defines such a profession or occupation as either certifying or licensing, as follows:

A self-regulating profession or occupation can be of two kinds. It may be a certifying body, in which case it has the right to confer a designation called a reserved title, which by law cannot be used by an unauthorized person. Certification is an important signal to members of the public that an individual offering services to clients or to employers has achieved a stipulated level of training and practical experience. But it does not prevent uncertified individuals from offering similar services.

Quite distinct from a certifying body, a self-regulating profession can be a licensing body, in which case an unauthorized person is prevented by law, not only from using the given designation, but from offering licensed services. In each instance, a right has been conferred on a self-regulating profession by the Legislature. In the case of the licensing body, this right is particularly valuable in economic terms.

PROFESSIONAL ORGANIZATIONS—NON-LICENSING

Many notable professional societies are non-licensing. They function as conservatories of knowledge pertaining to the profession or to a branch of it, as forums for discussion and the setting of standards, as advocates of the profession in public affairs. Their reserved titles (as, in our profession, and taking examples from English-speaking countries, EIC, ASCE, I Mech E., IEEE, CIC, CIMM, et cetera) are, in the words of the POC Report, an important signal—doubly important where practice of the profession is not reserved to licensees, as in science, music, and so on, and thus no signal of exclusive right to practise appears.

PROFESSIONAL ORGANIZATIONS—LICENSING

The reserved title of a licensing body is a guarantee that the licensing body considers the holder of the title to have met certain standards of competence. This guarantee is given the more weight in public esteem where the conditions for the granting of the licence are known to be rigorous and to be set forth in the law under which the licensing body holds its privilege.

POWER OF CONTROL OF LICENSEES

The responsibility of declaring (implicitly) that a licensee is competent requires authority; authority requires a power of control, usually represented by the right to impose penalties for misconduct or for demonstrated incompetence. In our own Association, which is probably typical of self-regulating and licensing professional bodies (as distinct from state-regulated bodies), the power over its members (licensees) is that of reprimand, suspension or termination of the membership (licence). The Association does not, in its own right, have any power over any person who is not a member (licensee), and offences against the Professional Engineers Act by such a person can only be certified by the Association before the appropriate court of law.

MEMBER VS. LICENSEE

In the immediately foregoing paragraph we have shown the word "licensee" in brackets beside the word "member," indicating that what was said applied to either. The word "member" is in every-day use and has many meanings; the term "licensee," meaning one who holds a licence, is really more precise, in view of the following definition of "licence": a formal permission from a constituted authority to do something, for example, to marry, preach, carry on some trade, and so on. In Canada, however, the formal permission to practise engineering is an attribute of membership in the Association (or the Order, in Quebec) in each province. The Professional Engineers Act of Ontario, for instance, is worded throughout to agree with this usage, and the words "licence" and "licensee" are particularly used to designate the permission granted to, and the status of, a non-member who is allowed, usually in some limited matter, the privileges of a member. (Further explanation of this is given in this chapter under licensing, page 19.)

In the United States, engineers are licensed to practise and to use the reserved title "professional engineer" (written "P.E." or "R.P.E.") by a state board of registration. They are not members of the board, and their profession is not self-regulating but state regulated. They are known as licensees.

DESIGNATION AS A SPECIALIST (O.REG. 59/73)

It must be understood that members designated as specialists by the council do not enjoy an extension of the right to practise they already enjoy as members. They are granted an additional reserved title, "specialist" (in the class in which they have been

17

designated). In granting this reserved title, the council is acting only as a certifying body; holders of titles have two important signals by which the public may evaluate their competence.

DESIGNATION AS A CONSULTING ENGINEER (O.REG. 60/73)

Members designated by the council as consulting engineers do not enjoy an extension of the right to practise they are allowed as members, but they do hold an additional reserved title, "consulting engineer," as a second important signal (or a third, if they are also designated as specialists). The reserved title, however, may not be used if the member is not in independent practice as defined in the Regulation.

BRANCH OF REGISTRATION

Every member is registered as being in one of the following five branches of engineering; normally the branch is determined by the preponderant discipline of the member's education.

Chemical and Metallurgical
Civil
Electrical
Mechanical, Aeronautical and Industrial
Mining

PRACTICE IN A BRANCH OTHER THAN THAT OF REGISTRATION

The member's branch appears against his name in the directory of members, published periodically, but not upon his seal (Section 19 of the act). To the extent that the branch constitutes a signal it is only a partial one, for the member is not restricted in his right to practise by his branch of registration, except as the Code of Ethics 6(b) applies.

PROFESSIONALS AND TECHNICAL PERSONNEL

In matters related to work performed by non-members and non-licensees the Association administers the Act in accordance with what it considers to be the spirit of the Act in such matters; that is, in accordance with the policy stated in the following two paragraphs:

In general, work of a nonrecurring nature or work requiring a novel application of engineering principles may be delegated to persons who are not members or licensees of the Association only under the close and continuing personal direction and supervision of a member or licensee of the Association who has accepted responsibility for the engineering work in his capacity as a professional engineer.

Engineering work involving the routine application of well-known principles and procedures may be delegated to persons who are not members or licensees of the Association under the direction and supervision of the member or licensee of the Association who has accepted responsibility for the engineering work in his capacity as a professional engineer. The direction and supervision must be exercised at a level of care, skill and attention satisfactory to the responsible professional engineer and shall be such that he is able to maintain an adequate knowledge and control of the engineering work for which he has accepted responsibility as a professional engineer.

PARTNERSHIPS, CORPORATIONS

A partnership or corporation can act only as the persons it comprises, or the managers they elect, dictate. If, therefore, it is to be permitted to practise professional engineering in its own right, there must be at least one person of adequate standing within the partnership or corporation who, being a member or licensee of the Association, formally undertakes responsibility for and supervision of the practice of professional engineering by the partnership or corporation.

This formal undertaking is part of the form of application by which a Certificate of Authorization is requested of the association. The Certificate of Authorization is a permission for the partnership or corporation to practise in its own name to the full extent of the right to practise of the members or licensees who have signed the undertaking (see Professional Engineers Act, Section 20).

LICENSING

We have already mentioned that in the Professional Engineers Act, and in the usage of APEO (and of the other provincial associations), a licensee is one who, not being a member of the association, yet enjoys, to a limited extent and for a limited time, the right to practise professional engineering within the jurisdiction of the licensing association.

Thus, a person, partnership or corporation in Ontario can employ an engineer who is not a resident of Ontario and not a member of APEO to carry out a particular work in Ontario. Such licensees must have satisfied the APEO as to their personal competence, which, for residents of Canada elsewhere than in Ontario, requires that the licensees be members of one of the regulating bodies of the profession in the provinces and territories of Canada. Eligibility and competence, where the licensees are not residents of Canada, must have been proved to meet the qualifications set forth in Section 17(2) of the Professional Engineers Act, these being such as to reasonably guarantee that membership would have been available to the licensees had they been residents of Ontario.

A licence is issued to residents of Canada by the registrar and reported to council; council itself approves non-resident licences before they are issued. In the latter case, council may, if it sees fit, impose the condition that the work be done in collaboration with a member who shall have undertaken to co-sign and co-seal all drawings and documents relating to the work. (Section 17[6]).

THE PROFESSIONAL ENGINEERS ACT OF THE PROVINCE OF ONTARIO

The authors gratefully acknowledge permission of the Association to reproduce here these Sections from the Office Consolidation Edition of the Act, which was prepared in convenient form by the Association and is available at the APEO office. That edition was prepared for purposes of convenience only, and for accurate reference recourse should be had to the statutes. The sections included here are those that relate to the subject of this chapter—regulation of the profession.

It should be noted that, in accordance with the provisions of Sections 7, 8 and 9 of the Act, the council of the Association is authorized to establish and, from time to time, to amend the regulations, the by-laws and the Code of Ethics of the Association.

Revised Statutes of Ontario, 1970, Chapter 366 as amended by 1972, Sections 1, 2, 3, 9, 11, 12, 13, 17, 18, 19, 20 and 27 only.

INTERPRETATION

1. In this Act,
   (a) "Association" means the Association of Professional Engineers of the Province of Ontario;
   (b) "by-law" means a by-law of the Association;
   (c) "chapter" means a group of members constituted and governed by by-law;
   (d) "council" means the council of the Association;
   (e) "graduate" means a graduate of a university or other educational institution in a course in any branch of engineering or science, the practice of which constitutes professional engineering and which is recognized by the council;
   (f) "licence" means a licence to practise professional engineering issued under this Act;
   (g) "licensee" means a person who holds a subsisting licence;
   (h) "member" means a member of the Association;
   (i) "practice of professional engineering" means the doing of one or more acts of advising on, reporting on, designing of or supervising of the construction of all public utilities, industrial works, railways, tramways, bridges, tunnels, highways, roads, canals, harbour works, lighthouses, river improvements, wet docks, dry docks, floating docks, dredges, cranes, drainage works, irrigation works, waterworks, water purification plants, sewerage works, sewage disposal works, incinerators, hydraulic works, power transmission systems, steel, concrete or reinforced concrete structures, electric lighting systems, electric power plants, electric machinery, electric or electronic apparatus, electrical or electronic communications systems or equipment, mineral property, mining machinery, mining development, mining operations, gas or oil developments, smelters, refineries, metallurgical machinery or equipment or apparatus for carrying out such operations, machinery, boilers or their auxiliaries, steam engines, hydraulic turbines, pumps, internal combustion engines or other mechanical structures, chemical or metallurgical machinery, apparatus or processes, or

aircraft, and generally all other engineering works including the engineering works and installations relating to airports, airfields or landing strips or relating to town and community planning;

(j) "professional engineer" means a person who is a member or licensee;

(k) "region" means a geographical area of Ontario as defined by by-law;

(l) "register" means the record of registrants maintained by the registrar;

(m) "registrant" means a person recorded in the register as a member, licensee, an assistant to a professional engineer, a graduate or an undergraduate;

(n) "registrar" means the registrar of the Association;

(o) "regulation" means a regulation of the Association;

(p) "undergraduate" means a student enrolled at but not graduated from a university or other educational institution in a course in any branch of engineering or science the practice of which constitutes professional engineering and that is recognized by the council. R.S.O. 1970, c. 366, s. 1.

2. Activities not affected—Nothing in this Act prevents,

(a) any person from performing his duties in the Canadian Armed Forces;

(b) any member or licensee of the Ontario Association of Architects under The Architects Act or any employee of such member or licensee acting under the direction and responsibility of such member or licensee from performing professional engineering services in the course of any work undertaken or proposed to be undertaken by such member or licensee as an architect; R.S.O. 1970, c. 27.

(c) any person who holds a certificate of qualification under The Operating Engineers Act from practising or designating himself as an operating engineer; R.S.O. 1970, c. 27.

(d) any person from practising as a bacteriologist, chemist, geologist, mineralogist or physicist;

(e) any person from advising on or reporting on any mineral property or prospect;

(f) any person from operating, executing or supervising any works as owner, contractor, superintendent, foreman, inspector or master,

or requires any such person to become registered or licensed under this Act in order to do any such thing. R.S.O. 1970. c. 366, s. 2.

3. Association continued—(1) The body politic and corporate known as the "Association of Professional Engineers of the Province of Ontario" incorporated under The Professional Engineers Act, 1922 is hereby continued. 1922, c. 59.

(2) All persons who were members of the Association on the 1st day of August, 1969 or who have been admitted as members since that day constitute the Association.

(3) The objects of the Association are,

    (a) to regulate the practice of professional engineering and to govern the profession in accordance with this Act, the regulations and the by-laws;

    (b) to establish and maintain standards of knowledge and skill among its members; and

    (c) to establish and maintain standards of professional ethics among its members,

in order that the public interest may be served and protected. R.S.O. 1970, c. 366, s. 3(1-3).

(4) The head office of the Association shall be in the Municipality of Metropolitan Toronto. 1972, c. 45, s. 1.

(5) The Association may purchase, acquire or take by gift, devise or bequest for the purposes of the Association and furtherance of its objects, but for no other purposes or objects, any real or personal property, and may sell, mortgage, lease or otherwise dispose of any such property. R.S.O. 1970, c. 366, s. 3(5).

9.   (1) The council shall prepare and publish from time to time a code of ethics containing standards of conduct designed for the protection of the public, which standards members and licensees must subscribe to and follow in the practice of professional engineering.

(2) copies of the code of ethics shall be sent to the members and licensees and shall be available free of charge to members of the public who apply therefor. R.S.O. 1970, c. 366, s. 9.

10.   CCPE The council may authorize participation by the Association in the activities of the Canadian Council of Professional Engineers, as a constituent association thereof. R.S.O. 1970, c. 366, s. 10.

MEMBERSHIP

11.   Qualification for membership—(1) any applicant for membership who,

    (a) resides,

        (i) in Ontario,

       (ii) out of Ontario and is employed for an indefinite period as a full-time employee of an employer having works or facilities in Ontario and is required by the terms of his employment to practise professional engineering in respect of such works or facilities or has a place of employment in Ontario and practises or proposes to practise professional engineering in Ontario on a full-time basis;

(b) is twenty-one or more years of age;

(c) has passed the examinations prescribed by the council or is exempted therefrom pursuant to subsection 3;

(d) has had six or more years of experience in engineering work satisfactory to council; and

(e) provides satisfactory evidence of good character,

shall be admitted as a member by the council.

(2) Evidence of qualification—Each applicant for membership shall submit upon the prescribed form evidence of his educational qualifications and engineering experience, information as to his residence and at least three references as to his character and engineering experience, and he may be required by the council to verify the statements set out in his application by affidavit.

(3) Credit for academic and other qualifications . . . The council may exempt an applicant from any of the examinations mentioned in clause c of subsection 1 if the council is of the opinion that the applicant has adequate academic and other qualifications.

(4) Credit for time spent at a university—Where the applicant is a graduate, upon presenting evidence of the actual time during which he was under instruction as an undergraduate in a university, the council shall grant him the time spent under such instruction in reduction of the six-year period of engineering experience required by clause d of subsection 1, but only in so far as the total exemption granted does not exceed four years.

(5) The council may for the purpose of subsection 3 or 4 require the board of examiners to consider and make recommendations to the council with respect to any application for exemption, including an application for exemption of a graduate in honours science. R.S.O. 1970, c. 366, s. 11.

12. Admission of members of other associations—The council may, upon application and satisfactory proof of residence, admit as a member any person who resides in Ontario, or who resides out of Ontario under the circumstances set out in subclause ii of clause a of subsection 1 of section 11, and who furnishes satisfactory proof,

(a) that he is a member of an association of professional engineers in another province or a territory of Canada that has objects similar to those of the Association and requirements for membership no less exacting than those in effect in Ontario; or

(b) that he is a member of an association of professional engineers in another part of the Commonwealth or in the United States of America that has objects similar to those of the Association and requirements no less exacting than those in effect in Ontario. R.S.O. 1970, c. 366, s. 12.

13.   Students and assistants

(1) Persons who are engaged as assistants to professional engineers in categories recognized by the council and graduates and undergraduates who have not completed the period of engineering experience required by this Act and who contemplate applying for membership on the completion of the period of engineering experience may, upon application in the prescribed form, be recorded in the register but not as members of the Association until fully qualified, and upon being so recorded are subject to the control of the council in accordance with this Act, the regulations and the by-laws.

(2) Deletion of names—Any registrant whose name is recorded in the register pursuant to subsection 1 may, upon application, have his name deleted from the register. R.S.O. 1970, c. 366, s. 13.

LICENSING

17.   Issue of licences to members of associations of other provinces—

(1) The registrar may upon application issue a licence to any person who resides in Canada but not in Ontario and who furnishes satisfactory proof that he is a member of an association of professional engineers in another province or a territory of Canada that has objects similar to those of the Association.

(2) Issue of licences to consulting specialists—Any person who does not reside in Canada but who in the opinion of the council is a consulting specialist in a field of professional engineering who has had not less than ten years experience in the practice of his profession, or who furnishes satisfactory evidence that he has qualifications at least equal to those required for registration as a professional engineer in Ontario, may, with the approval of the council, be issued a licence.

(3) Issue of licences to persons from provinces without associations—Any person practising or proposing to practise professional engineering in Ontario who resides in a province or territory of Canada in which there is no association of professional

engineers that has objects similar to those of the Association, may, with the approval of the council, be issued a licence.

(4) Practise by applicant for a licence—Where an applicant for a licence fails to obtain it promptly for any reason unrelated to his professional capacity or his own neglect, he may practise professional engineering in Ontario for a period of not more than three months without a licence.

(5) The registrar shall issue a licence in the prescribed form to any person entitled thereto and shall specify therein the work upon which and the name of the employer in Ontario by whom the holder of the licence is to be employed and the period for which it is issued, but in no case shall the period extend beyond the end of the calendar year in which the licence is issued.

(6) The council may direct that any licence issued under subsection 2 shall, in addition to the conditions mentioned in subsection 5, contain a condition that the licensee may practise professional engineering in Ontario only in collaboration with a member who shall sign and seal any plans and specifications together with the licensee. R.S.O. 1970, c. 366, s. 17.

18.   Where licence not required—Any person who is employed as a professional engineer by a public service corporation carrying on an interprovincial undertaking or by the Government of Canada and who is by reason of his employment required to practise professional engineering in a province or territory of Canada other than that of his residence may practise professional engineering in Ontario without a license, but he shall on demand of the council furnish satisfactory evidence that he is a member of an association of professional engineers in another province or a territory of Canada that has objects similar to those of the Association. R.S.O. 1970, c. 366, s. 18.

19.   Seals, members—

(1) Every member shall have a seal of a design approved by the council, the impression of which shall contain the name of the engineer and the words "Registered Professional Engineer" and "Province of Ontario".

(2) Idem, Licensees—Every licensee shall have a seal of a design approved by the council, the impression of which shall contain the name of the licensee and the words "Licensed Professional Engineer" and "Province of Ontario".

(3) Signature and use of seal—All final drawings, specifications, plans, reports and other documents involving the practice of professional engineering when issued shall bear the signature and seal of the professional engineer who prepared or approved them.

R.S.O. 1970, c. 366, s. 19.

PARTNERSHIPS, CORPORATIONS

20. Practice prohibited by partnerships and corporations—

(1) No partnership, association of persons or corporation as such shall be a member or a licensee, or shall, except as authorized by this section, practise professional engineering.

(2) A partnership association of persons or corporation that holds a certificate of authorization may, in its own name, practise professional engineering.

   (a) if one of its principal or customary functions is to engage in the practice of professional engineering; and

   (b) if the practice of professional engineering is done under the responsibility and supervision of a member of the partnership or association of persons, or of a director or full-time employee of the corporation, as the case may be, who,

   (i) is a member, or

   (ii) is a licensee, in which case the practice of professional engineering shall be restricted to the work specified in the licence of the licencee.

(3) A partnership, association of persons or corporation that desires a certificate of authorization shall submit to the registrar an application in the prescribed form containing,

   (a) the names and addresses of all its partners, members, officers or directors, as the case may be;

   (b) the names of all its partners, members of associations of persons, directors of corporations, or full-time employees of corporations, as the case may be, who are the members or licensees who will be in charge of professional engineering on its behalf;

   (c) from among the names specified under clause b the name or names of its official representative or representatives whose duty it is to ensure that this Act, and the regulations and the by-laws are complied with by the partnership, the association of persons or the corporation, as the case may be,

and shall, whenever there is a change in the particulars given in its application, give notice of the change to the registrar within thirty days after the effective date of the change.

(4) If subsection 3 is complied with, the registrar shall issue to the applicant a certificate of authorization.

(5) Where the holder of a certificate of authorization ceases to have any official representative, the certificate is ipso facto revoked, and the partnership, association of persons or corporation shall not practise professional engineering until a new certificate of authorization is issued.

(6) Where the council finds that the holder of a certificate of authorization has failed to observe any of the provisions of this section or has been guilty of conduct that would, in the case of a member or licensee, have been professional misconduct, the council may reprimand the holder or suspend or revoke the certificate of authorization.

(7) Sections 24, 25 and 26 apply mutatis mutandis to the refusal to issue a certificate of authorization and to the revocation or suspension of a certificate of authorization. R.S.O. 1970, c. 366, s. 20.

OFFENCES

27. (1) Every person, other than a member or a licensee, who,

  (a) takes and uses orally or otherwise the title ''Professional Engineer'' or ''Registered Professional Engineer'' or uses any addition to or abbreviation of either such titles, or any word, name or designation that will lead to the belief that he is a professional engineer, a member or a licensee or, except as permitted by section 2, uses the title or designation ''engineer'' in such a manner as will lead to the belief that he is a professional engineer, a member or a licensee;

  (b) advertises, holds himself out, or conducts himself in any way or by any means as a member or a licensee; or

  (c) engages in the practice of professional engineering,

is guilty of an offence.

(2) Every person who,

  (a) wilfully procures or attempts to procure registration under this Act for himself or for another person by making, producing or causing to be made or produced any fraudulent representation or declaration either verbal or written; or

  (b) knowingly makes any false statement in any application or declaration signed or filed by him under this Act,

is guilty of an offence.

(3) Where a partnership, association of persons or corporation that has no subsisting certificate of authorization,

  (a) practices professional engineering;

  (b) uses orally or otherwise any name, title, description or designation that will lead to the belief that it is entitled to practice professional engineering; or

  (c) advertises, holds itself out or conducts itself in any way or in such manner as to lead to the belief that it is entitled to practise professional engineering,

every member of the partnership, every member of the association or persons, or the corporation and every director thereof, is guilty of an offence.

(4) Where a partnership, association of persons or corporation that has a subsisting certificate of authorization practises professional engineering in contravention of the act, every member of the partnership, every member of the association of persons, or the corporation and every director thereof, is guilty of an offence.

(5) Penalties—Every person, member of a partnership, member of an association of persons, and every corporation and director thereof, who is guilty of an offence under this section is on summary conviction liable to a fine of not more than $1,000. or to imprisonment for a term of not more than six months, or to both.

(6) Limitation of proceedings—No proceeding shall be commenced for a contravention of any of the provisions of this section after two years from the date of the commission of such contravention. R.S.O. 1970, c. 366, s. 27.

BY-LAW NO. 2

Procedure on Application for Membership.

BE IT ENACTED as a by-law of the Association of Professional Engineers of the Province of Ontario (hereinafter called the "Association") as follows:

1. Application for admission as a member under Section 11 of the Act shall be submitted to the Association.
2. The Association shall advise each applicant for membership of the examinations, if any, which he is required to pass.
3. (1) The Board of Examiners shall consist of a chairman, a vice-chairman, and such other members as the Council may determine from time to time.
   (2) Applications may be referred to the Board of Examiners for assessment of academic qualifications and recommendations to Council with respect to the examinations prescribed for such applicants.
   (3) The Board of Examiners may interview any applicants for membership referred to it by the Council, or by the registrar, or who have submitted further evidence justifying a review of their academic qualifications. The Board shall review the qualifications of applicants in the light of the standards for admission to membership currently established.
   (4) The Board of Examiners shall make recommendations to Council with respect to the examinations prescribed by Council for applicants for membership and shall arrange

29

for the setting of, and approve, the papers for such examinations.

4. (1) The Council may appoint annually a committee, to be known as the Appeal Board, consisting of a chairman, a vice-chairman, and such other members as the Council may determine from time to time.

   (2) If the educational qualifications of an applicant for membership have been found to be deficient in engineering subjects required for full exemption from the examinations prescribed by the Council, and if such applicant has academic qualifications in a field of science, or has had experience of such length or such record of accomplishment and level of responsibility in a field of engineering, as to indicate that his qualifications in these respects are significantly in excess of the minimum requirements of the Act, the application of such applicant may be referred to the Appeal Board for review.

   (3) The Appeal Board may interview all applicants for membership referred to it by the Council or by the registrar or who have made application for such interview, shall consider the qualifications of such applicant by assessing the educational deficiencies in engineering subjects in the light of the qualifications of the applicant in excess of the minimum requirements in other respects, and shall make recommendations to the Council.

5. (1) The Council may appoint annually a committee to be known as the Professional Interviewing Committee, consisting of a chairman, vice-chairman, and such other members as the Council may determine from time to time.

   (2) If the academic training of an applicant for membership has been conducted in a language other than English or French, or if a question requiring clarification has been raised by the references or by another reliable source as to the character and engineering experience submitted by the applicant or otherwise in connection with his application, the registrar may refer the applicant to the Professional Interviewing Committee for further consideration.

   (3) The Professional Interviewing Committee shall interview all applicants referred to it by the registrar and shall make recommendations to the Council.

O. REG. 59/73—DESIGNATION OF SPECIALISTS

1. (1) Any applicant for specialist designation who,

     (a) is a member;

   (b) is currently engaged in the practice of professional engineering or is teaching at a level and at an institution that are satisfactory to the Council, a course in any branch of engineering or science, the practice of which constitutes professional engineering and that is recognized by the Council or is otherwise engaged at such an institution in an office or position satisfactory to the Council, in the Province of Ontario;

   (c) has had five or more years of experience beyond membership requirements satisfactory to the Council in the field of engineering in respect of which designation as a specialist is being sought; and

   (d) has passed the examinations prescribed by the Council or has been exempted therefrom, pursuant to subsection 2,

shall be designated by the Council as a specialist in that field of engineering.

(2) The Council may exempt an applicant from any of the examinations mentioned in clause d of subsection 1 if the Council is of the opinion that the applicant has adequate experience, technical competence, academic qualifications and other qualifications.

(3) The Council shall forwith after reaching a decision mail to an applicant, postage prepaid, addressed to his last address appearing on the register, written notice that he has or has not been designated a specialist, as the case may be, as applied for, and where a member has been designated a specialist, the Council shall specify the title, term or designation by which such specialist may indicate his specialization in a field of engineering. O. Reg. 59 /73, s. 1.

An application may be for specialist designation in one or more fields of engineering or for more than one specialist designation within any field of engineering. O. Reg. 59 /73, s. 2.

3. The Council may appoint a board of specialization to make recommendations to the Council with respect to all matters relating to applications for specialist designation and for requalification for specialist designation, as provided for in section 5, and, without limiting the generality of the foregoing,

   (a) respecting the standards to be applied;

   (b) respecting procedure for, and the make-up of, examinations;

   (c) respecting the qualifications of applicants; and

(d) respecting exemption of applicants from examinations. O. Reg. 59/73, s. 3.

4. An applicant shall appear personally before the Council or, if a board of specialization has been appointed, the board of specialization, when so requested. O. Reg. 59/73, s. 4.

5. Designation as a specialist shall, unless earlier revoked pusuant to section 9, be valid for a period of five years, at which time application for requalification may be made. O. Reg. 59/73, s. 5.

6. Section 1 shall apply mutatis mutandis to any application for requalification as a specialist. O. Reg. s. 6.

7. (1) Any applicant whom the Council has refused to designate as a specialist may, within thirty days from the date upon which he receives written notice of such refusal under subsection 3 of section 1, request the Council to reconsider his application, and upon receipt of such request the Council shall reconsider the application, taking into account such additional evidence, if any, as is submitted by the applicant.

   (2) An applicant shall be deemed to have received such written notification on the second business day after it has been mailed to him, postage prepaid, addressed to his last address appearing on the register.

   (3) Upon any hearing conducted under this section, the Council may make findings of fact by such standards of proof as are commonly relied upon by reasonable and prudent men in the conduct of their own affairs.

   (4) The Council shall forthwith after reaching a decision on any application for reconsideration mail to the applicant, postage prepaid, addressed to his last address appearing on the register, written notice either confirming the prior refusal of specialist designation or advising that such applicant has been designated a specialist, as the case may be, and, in the latter event, specifying the title, term or designation by which such applicant may indicate his specialization. O. Reg. 59/73, s. 7.

8. Only a member who has been designated as such by the Council may take and use the term, title or designation denoting his qualifications as a specialist in a field of engineering; use of any term, title or designation that will lead to the belief that he has been designated as a specialist by a member not so designated will constitute improper conduct in a professional respect under the definition of "professional misconduct" in the regulations. O. Reg. 59/73, s. 8.

9. Designation as a specialist may be revoked if the specialist

has been found guilty of professional misconduct under section 25 of the Act. O. Reg. 59/73, s. 9.

10. The Council may, from time to time, establish fees with respect to the designation of specialists. O. Reg. 59/73, s. 10.

11. The Council shall cause to be published annually listings of members designated specialists. O. Reg. 59/73, s. 11.

12. Where the Council has notified an applicant under subsection 3 of section 1 on under subsection 4 of section 7 that he has not been designated a specialist as applied for, such applicant shall not be entitled to re-apply for such specialist designation for a period of twelve months from the date of such notification. O. Reg. 59 /73, s. 12.

13. There shall be the following classes of specialists in the various fields of engineering:

Fields of Engineering	Classes of Specialists
Civil:	Structures
	Transportation
	Environmental
	Geotechnics
	Hydraulics
	Other Civil Engineering specialist classes
Mechanical:	Mechanics
	Industrial
	Production
	Power
	Heating and Air Conditioning
	Other Mechanical Engineering specialist classes
Aerospace:	Structures
	Aerodynamics
	Propulsion
	Other Aerospace Engineering specialist classes
Electrical:	Power
	Electronics
	Communications and Control
	Other Electrical Engineering specialist Classes
Chemical:	Processes
	Production
	Control

	Other Chemical Engineering specialist classes
Metallurgical:	Mineral Processing and Extraction Materials Other Metallurgical Engineering specialist classes
Mining:	Methods and Systems Processing Other Mining Engineering specialist classes
Geological:	Exploration Development Other Geological Engineering specialist classes
Agricultural and Biological:	Food Production Food Processing Forestry Other Agricultural and Biological Engineering specialist classes

O. Reg. 59/73, s. 13.

O. REG. 60/73—CONSULTING ENGINEERS

1. (1) Any applicant for designation as a consulting engineer who,

    (a) is a member;

    (b) is currently engaged in the practice of professional engineering in the Province of Ontario;

    (c) has had five or more years of experience in the practice of professional engineering, beyond membership requirements, satisfactory to the Council; and

    (d) has passed the examinations prescribed by the Council or has been exempted therefrom, pursuant to subsection 2,

shall be designated by the Council as a consulting engineer.

(2) The Council may exempt an applicant from any of the examinations mentioned in clause (d) of subsection 1 if the Council is of the opinion that the applicant has adequate experience, technical competence, academic qualifications and other qualifications.

(3) The Council shall forthwith after reaching a decision mail to an applicant, postage prepaid, addressed to his last

address appearing on the register, written notice that he has or has not been designated as a consulting engineer, as the case may be, and where a member has been so designated he may take and use the title "Consulting Engineer" or any appropriate variation thereof approved by the Council at such time or times as he is in independent practice.

(4) For the purpose of this Regulation, a member shall be deemed to be in independent practice if,

    (a) he offers professional engineering services generally to the public;

    (b) he is a member of a partnership or association of persons or an officer or director of a corporation and such partnership, association of persons or corporation offers professional engineering services generally to the public; or

    (c) he is a full-time employee of a member mentioned in clause (a) or of a partnership, association of persons or corporation mentioned in clause (b). O. Reg. 60/73, s. 1.

The Council may appoint a board of regulation to make recommendations to the Council with respect to all matters relating to applications for designation as a consulting engineer and for requalification as such, as provided for in section 4, and, without limiting the generality of the foregoing,

    (a) respecting the standards to be applied;

    (b) respecting procedures for and the make-up of, examinations;

    (c) respecting the qualifications of applicants, and

    (d) respecting exemption of applicants from examinations. O. Reg. 60/73, s. 2.

3. An applicant shall appear personally before the Council or, if a board of regulation has been appointed, the board of regulation, when so requested. O. Reg. 60/73, s. 3.

4. Designation as a consulting engineer shall, unless earlier revoked pursuant to section 8, be valid for a period of five years, at which time application for requalification may be made. O. Reg. 60/73, s. 4.

5. Section 1 shall apply mutatis mutandis to any application for requalification as a consulting engineer. O. Reg. 60/73, s. 5.

6. (1) Any applicant whom the Council has refused to designate as a consulting engineer may, within thirty days from the date upon which he receives written notice of such refusal under subsection 3 of section 1, request the Coun-

35

cil to reconsider his application, and upon receipt of such requests the Council shall reconsider the application, taking into account such additional evidence, if any, as is submitted by the applicant.

(2) An applicant shall be deemed to have received such written notification on the second business day after it has been mailed to him, postage prepaid, addressed to his last address appearing on the register.

(3) Upon any hearing conducted under this section, the Council may make findings of fact by such by such standards of proof as are commonly relied upon by reasonable and prudent ment in the conduct of their own affairs.

(4) The Council shall forthwith after reaching a decision on any application for reconsideration mail to the applicant, postage prepaid, addressed to his last address appearing on the register, written notice either confirming the prior refusal of designation as a consulting engineer or advising that such applicant has been designated as a consulting engineer, as the case may be. O. Reg. 60/73, s. 6.

7. Only those persons who have been designated as such by the Council may take and use the title ''Consulting Engineer'' or any appropriate variation thereof approved by the Council; use of such title or such variation by a member not so designated, by a partnership, association of persons or corporation at a time when it is not entitled to do so under section 10 or by a member who is so designated but at a time when he is not in independent practice will constitute improper conduct in a professional respect under the definition of ''professional misconduct'' in the regulations. O. Reg. 60/73, s. 7.

8. Designation as a consulting engineer may be revoked if the consulting engineer has been found guilty of professional misconduct under section 25 of the Act. O. Reg. 60/73, s. 8.

9. The council may, from time to time, establish fees with respect to the designation of consulting engineers. O. Reg. 60/73, s. 9.

10. A partnership, association of persons or corporation that holds a certificate of authorization may use the title ''Consulting Engineers'' or any appropriate variation thereof approved by the Council, where the practice of professional engineering is done under the responsibility and supervision of a designated consulting engineer who is in independent practice. O. Reg. 60/73, s. 10.

11. The right of a partnership, association of persons or corpora-

tion to use the title "Consulting Engineers" or any variation thereof under section 10 may be revoked if the partnership, association of persons or corporation has been found guilty of conduct that would, in the case of a member or licensee, have been professional misconduct under section 25 of the Act. O. Reg. 60/73, s. 11.

12. The Council shall cause to be published annually a listing of members designated as consulting engineers and of partnerships, associations of persons and corporations entitled to use the title "Consulting Engineers" or any variation thereof. O. Reg. 60/73, s. 12.

13. A member may only make one application for designation as a consulting engineer in any twelve-month period. O. Reg. 60/73, s. 13.

14. This Regulation comes into force on the 1st day of January, 1974, O. Reg. 60/73, s. 14.

The Experience Requirement for Registration, 10 pages D.S. and Notes 1, 2 & 3.

THE EXPERIENCE REQUIREMENT FOR REGISTRATION

An applicant who has completed the working-experience requirement of a professional regulating authority may certainly be held to have gained at least something of three tangible benefits: command of practical skills appropriate to an engineer (and for the most part not subjects of instruction in the universities); familiarity with some branch of industry and, in general, with commercial customs; practice of professional engineering under supervision.

In the eighteenth and nineteenth centuries, the novice who had completed a pupilage (apprenticeship) under a practitioner should have acquired the same benefits plus an additional benefit: an engineering education, of which the substance was whatever the practitioner thought desirable, or whatever the practitioner was willing and able to provide. Today's working-experience requirement survives from the apprenticeship system. It is a training process completely separate from the academic, the burden of formal education in engineering having been shifted to the schools.[1] It is intended to preserve what was good in the pupilage system—skills, familiarity with industry and commerce, work under practitioners. It is the last of these that concerns us most in discussing professional ethics.

37

The standards of ethical behaviour of two hundred years ago were set by individual practitioners, who were for the most part "ingenious mechanics," as C. R. Young put it.[2] The pupil, therefore, had as an example an application of personal ethics; examples must have varied in quality between good and bad depending on the character of the practitioner to whom the student was articled. For better or for worse in this respect, the contact was prolonged; periods approaching ten years were not uncommon in these indentures. Today's professional engineers work with conscious observance of a code of ethics, but the required period of contact of the engineer-in-training with the practitioner is comparatively brief. Registering authorities may therefore be expected to scan carefully this aspect of a record of experience submitted for consideration.

Fortunately, the schools provide a valuable association between the student and the teaching staff, most of the members of which are professionally qualified. At a time far enough removed from student days to give us a fair perspective, we recall such associations (happily, for the most part), and we realize from time to time that in the structures of vertical thinking between first principles and consummation of the level attained and in the lateral sowing of speculative thought, we were generally treated as if we were already the "other professional engineers" of canon five of the code, and that the teaching and manners to which we were subjected were intended to, and did, convey more than instruction in technological argument, even to the point of unspoken suggestion of canon one. Nevertheless, in an experience record, it is the presence of a reasonable contact with professional engineers in the working environment rather than in the academic environment that is normally demanded.

There used to be certain skills expected of the graduate engineer, presumably to be further developed during his period of working experience: many of us covered what seems to have been, looking back, an acreage of buff drawing paper at school; we became exponents of elaborate slide-rule mystique; we could consult the Carnegie handbook with one thumb while operating a pencil with the other hand; we would as soon (as one professor who liked to employ the picturesque in his analogies put it) have been caught without our trousers as without a steam-table in our possession.[3] Not so much importance is given today to such ancient virtues. A wide range of new and sophisticated skills, more specialized as to branch of practice, exists. Computer-aided design (CAD) has largely dispensed with the buff paper; factual information is likely to be drawn from the electronic memory. The acquisition or the polishing up of skills is not likely to be closely assessed as a constituent of experience for registration; that it exists will probably be taken as implied by the job description and the concurrent professional engineer associations.

The aspect of experience prior to registration we have spoken of as familiarity with industry and commercial customs is similarly likely to be considered as an implication of the job description; probably the important thing is that the activities devoted to this benefit be not excessive. There are induction courses in some large industrial companies where service in a succession of departments is the routine, where the process is not confined to engineers in training or those eligible for training status, but includes persons of comparable education in unallied fields, where the process is directed by a personnel department, and where final assignment to a particular department is by aptitude discovered or by the new employee's choice. Such courses are likely to be carefully scrutinized by a registering authority as warranting acceptance as engineering work, even if the final election be engineering. Where induction courses are under the aegis of the engineering department and are solely undergone prior to occupying positions in engineering, the situation is different. In industry, the engineer works in collaboration with departments other than his or her own; the engineers in training who accept that the code of ethics applies to themselves before registration just as it will afterwards owe ''fairness and loyalty to associates'' and must acquire a reasonable knowledge of who they are and what they do.

What has so far been said in this chapter indicates that, in the opinion of your authors, the most important element in an experience record is that it shall show substantial working contact with one or more professional engineers. There may be conventions followed by some regulating bodies that amount to something closer to a definition on this ground than ''substantial contact,'' but we are unaware of it; neither, considering the enormous range of engineer-in-training activities, does it seem to us possible that anything less than detailed consideration by the regulating body of each experience submission can be brought to its acceptance, partial acceptance or rejection.

Partial acceptance simply means that some allowance has been made for what has been submitted, leaving an outstanding period to which some condition may be attached for the guidance of the applicant. A rejection will presumably be accompanied by advice to the applicant as to the likelihood of the employment's ever providing eligible experience. Rejection does not impose a stigma; if the submission reveals contravention of the Professional Engineers Act (that is, unlicensed practice of professional engineering), the applicant will of course be warned to cease and desist; but there is an element of the traditional confessional in the engineer's provision of information, and it seems impossible to believe that a document so submitted would be used as evidence for prosecution connected with an offence committed prior to the submission and the issue of the warning arising from it.

An engineer-in-training, as the term is used here, based on Ontario custom, is a person who, having applied for this status or for membership, is educationally eligible but has not fulfilled the experience requirement. The status cannot be held for more than something of the order of five years (in Ontario). Nevertheless, provided the engineer's education continues to meet the requirement, the status can be renewed with a new application; if the educational requirement has changed at the time of such a new application, the candidate may have to update what was previously acceptable. The point is that rejection of an experience submission does not preclude subsequent steps towards registration. This limited time as engineer-in-training affects persons who may (often for good, sometimes for altruistic, reasons) plan to delay entering engineering work after graduation. It is not necessary to apply for engineer-in-training status immediately after graduation. The regulating authority should be consulted when such plans are being made.

"Substantial" can be a mighty insubstantial adjective; whatever it is applied to will have to be located by someone as a point in a scale of acceptability. Extremes in professional contact in engineering work are easy to imagine: from the safe circumstances of the engineer-in-training employed by a firm of consulting engineers or in the properly constituted engineering department of an industrial concern, we go to the difficult case of one who is doing engineering work entirely without professional tutelage[4] (which might occur legitimately, for instance, in Ontario, in the execution of works under Section 2[f] of The Professional Engineers Act, as, perhaps, in a family business). The intermediate range, in which many experience submissions lie, represents occasional, indirect or remote contact with professionals. Applicants who find themselves somewhere in this intermediate range, and forewarned, should set about improving the closeness and frequency of such contacts. They should participate to the full in whatever extramural activities of engineers they are entitled by their training status to attend, whether these are meetings, delivery of papers or bean-feasts, for often, when candidates seek references from professional engineers to accompany their experience submissions, they find themselves all but unknown to those they approach, and can get no more than a sort of hearsay recommendation. More important, the engineers within the candidate's own company should be visited periodically as a tactful reminder of the engineer-in-training's presence and of the fact that the candidate will be citing one or more of them as referees. There is no conscientious professional engineer who will not take this seriously (indeed, the training of successors is an ancient obligation of professionalism, as old, at least, as the Hippocratic Oath) and keep a weather eye on the engineer-in-training's work and progress so that the professional may speak knowledgeably when the time comes. Even where there are no engineers employed, a request should be made of the management, with an explanation of the reason, to participate in dealings with consulting engineers where these are retained. If, as is likely, the engineer-in-training has been taken on the strength of future engineering potential, the employer, if he understands the necessity for it, should co-operate in this in his own interests. One way or another, remote contact has to be maximized, and there is reason to believe that many applicants whose registration has been delayed on grounds of experience have not made thoughtful efforts to bring this about.

Decisions on experience gained abroad may be deferred for lack of adequate information; it is difficult to visualize, from a few facts, circumstances where firms, persons and customs are not known. In proportion to the risk of such delay, applicants should be meticulous about what is provided. An original testimonial of an employer showing dates and the title of the position held is desirable; the nature and magnitude of the employer's operations may be quite unknown to the registering authority and may have to be manifested by published matter; information about engineers cited as contacts with the profession will have to be complete enough to enable judgement whether these possess acceptable qualifications as professional engineers, since there are many parts of the world, including some states of the United

States insofar as employee engineers are concerned, where a person may be doing legally work that would be reserved to professional engineers in any of the Canadian provinces. Where an unregistered person outside of Canada is named as a referee of professional-engineer standing, the applicant, already enjoined to give information about the person so named, might find, in the requirements for temporary licence in the jurisdiction in which he is applying, a guide to the specific information he should supply. For Ontario, Section 17(2) of The Professional Engineers Act may be referred to. Your authors are not aware of any precedent or custom governing the recognition of non-registered persons as referees of professional standing (as, indeed, they are unaware of precedent or custom governing any aspect of judgement of experience records beyond the most straightforward); they have simply assumed here that, since a licensee has the standing of a professional engineer for the stipulated work of the licence, qualifications that would warrant the issue of a licence would be held sufficient to guarantee the standing of a person as a professional for the purpose of writing a recommendation.

Engineers frequently move into areas of activity that are not, under the law obtaining in their jurisdiction, or to be inferred from it, reserved to the professional engineer. Generally, these will have qualified for registration during a period of conventional engineering employment; the change, perhaps gradual, has occurred in relative maturity. There are, however, those who, immediately after graduation, or at any rate before the stipulated experience period has been completed, enter such employment. An experience submission under these circumstances will presumably face two questions: is it engineering work and are professional-engineer associations connected with it?

As to the first question, the border between engineering and pure science, applied mathematics, aspects of modern management, financial administration and so on seems to be increasingly indefinite, and strict adherence to the range of work reserved by law to the profession in judging what is engineering work is probably unlikely; in fact, if the second question is adequately answered—that is, if professional engineers are widely participating in the sort of work involved and the applicant can show substantial working contact with these—it seems fair to suppose that a reasonably good case exists. Perhaps pure-management occupations are the most doubtful and these should be most carefully and without exaggeration outlined in the submission.

Avoided should be the style employed in a case made known to your authors of a young real-estate development manager (of identity not divulged to them) who offered as evidence for registration that he was on "a fast track promotionwise" and "hired engineers when they were needed"!

In this matter of interpretation of occupations not firmly within the scope of engineering, the applicant at least can be confident that the registering body to which he submits his experience resumés is not less modern than himself in awareness and outlook.

PROFESSIONALS AND TECHNICAL PERSONNEL

In July, 1976, APEO was informed by letter from the chairman of the Ontario Law Reform Commission that the attorney general for Ontario had recently requested the commission "to undertake a review of the legislation regulating lawyers, notaries, accountants, engineers and architects." Four of these groups are self-regulating professions, having organizations described (under Academy, Association earlier in this chapter) as licensing bodies; notaries are regulated by the provincial government.

About a year later, when the commission had carried out its study and submitted a report, the task of deciding what action to take was assigned to the Professional Organizations Committee (POC) appointed by the attorney general. The findings of that committee, after study, public hearings, consideration of briefs and deliberation are contained in the POC Report, April, 1980.

Because actions prompted by recommendations contained in that report could bring about important changes in the conduct of the affairs of APEO and other professional organizations, it is appropriate to comment briefly on the membership of the committee and on its findings.

The chairman was H. Allan Leal, Q.C., deputy attorney general for the province of Ontario, former chairman of the Ontario Law Reform Commission; the other two members were J. Alex Corry, Q.C., former principal of Queen's University, former dean of law, Queen's University, and J. Stefan Dupré, Ph.D., professor of political science, University of Toronto, former chairman, department of political economy, University of Toronto. In addition to the two particular affiliations noted for Allan Leal, Alex Cory and Stefan Dupré, each of these three gentlemen has a distinguished and enviable reputation in his own profession and career.

43

It is significant to note that, even though both lawyers and engineers were mentioned in the terms of reference to the POC, two lawyers were named to the committee but no engineer was included. This might or might not be judged to be discrimination depending on who makes the judgement. It is an indication, however, that even as a self-regulating body, the Association is subject to the laws and regulations of our society; and these are enacted by the legislature. The political process determines the makeup of the legislature, and in that body the engineering segment is under-represented in comparison with other groups, in particular the legal profession. There may be a lesson to be learned from these facts.

Many of the judicious arguments advanced and opinions expressed in the report, in particular those related to self regulation, are closely related to the subject of this book. One matter of continuing concern is the proper supervision and control of work done by a person who is not a member or a licensee of APEO. Chapter 4 of the POC Report discusses this subject with lucidity and with the authority arising from careful investigation. On page 2 of this ten-page chapter, we find:

> [There is] some confusion regarding the legal effect of the Professional Engineers Act. Subsection i of section 1 of the Act defines "the practice of professional engineering" as "the doing" of one or more of a number of specified engineering activities, and section 27 effectively reserves the right to practise professional engineering to members of the Association of Professional Engineers of Ontario (APEO). It has been argued, however, that many technical employees are engaging daily in the performance of engineering functions such as those listed in subsection i of section 1 of the Act, often under only the most nominal supervision or direction of a licensed professional engineer. The proponents of this argument have suggested that, in the context of the workplace, the Act is as frequently honoured in the breach as in the observance.

Some five pages of discussion follow, terminating in:

> The amendments we propose would legislatively embody the view of the APEO that the essence of professional practise lies in the professional's accountability to the licensing authority for the quality and integrity of any engineering work with which he is associated, rather than in the actual

performance of the work. Furthermore, they would also clearly legitimize de facto practices of substituting skilled technical personnel for professional according to the professional's confidence in the skill and experience of such personnel. Non-professional personnel would be insulated from potential prosecution for unauthorized practice so long as they did not violate Section 27 of the Act by engaging in engineering work in cases where a licensee had not assumed professional responsibility for such work or otherwise hold themselves out to the public as entitled to carry the designation of "professional engineer". Accordingly, we recommend that:

The Professional Engineers Act be amended so as to:

(a) provide that the performance of engineering work by persons who are not professional engineers shall not be a violation of the Act so long as a professional engineer is professionally responsible to the Association of Professional Engineers of Ontario for the maintenance of engineering standards in the performance of the work; and

(b) stipulate that nothing in the Act shall be construed so as to prevent:

    (i) any person from engaging in testing and inspection activities, and reporting thereon, provided that the specifications and standards involved have been prepared or approved by a professional engineer;

    (ii) any person from undertaking the design of special production machinery, equipment, or tools and dies for use in his or her employer's facilities in the production of the employer's products; and

    (iii) any person from engaging in the repair, maintenance, or operation of the equipment and facilities of his or her employer.

One other recommendation is made, with the purpose of placing an onus on an employer to ensure compliance with the amended Act, as follows:

The Professional Engineers Act should be amended so as to enable the Association of Professional Engineers of Ontario to seek from the Divisional Court a cease and desist order against any person who knowingly retains, employs, contracts with or otherwise engages someone who is not a professional engineer for the performance of any act or acts constituting the practice of professional engineering.

In matters related to work performed by non-members and non-licensees, the Association administers the Act in accordance with what it considers to be the spirit of the Act, that is, in accordance with the policy stated earlier in this chapter of this book (under Professionals and Technical Personnel).

There are provisions for periodic review and amendment of the Professional Engineers Act of the Province of Ontario, but it takes time. Even though many dedicated officers and other members of the Association have worked conscientiously on its recommendations ever since the POC Report was issued in April 1980 to determine what should be done to put them into effect, no amendment has been enacted as of August 1982. The mills of God grind slowly, yet they grind exceeding small.

NOTES

1. The first recorded move to establish engineering as an educational discipline was in 1775 when the now justly famous Ecole des Ponts et Chausées was established. The transfer of engineering education to the schools was slow. This arose:

   . . . in part from the ill-disguised hostility of those having to do with traditional literary and philosophical studies [but] rather more from the fact that the great majority of practising engineers, wedded as they were to the pupilage system, did not look upon the acquisition of theoretical knowledge as an essential part of a young man's training. The ground taken was that engineering was an art rather than a science. The educational foundation given in the schools of engineering was therefore deemed to be only mildly auxiliary. Even men of the eminence of Rankine and Fleeming Jenkin were sometimes spoken of as "hypothetical engineers."

   C. R. Young, *Early Engineering Education at Toronto, 1851-1919* (University of Toronto Press, 1958).

2. C. R. Young was an eminent Canadian civil engineer, who was on the teaching staff of the University of Toronto from 1908 to 1949, for the final eight years as Dean of the Faculty of Applied Science and Engineering.

3. The story (no doubt apocryphal) is that the professor, further on in his lecture, asked for the loan of a steam-table.

4. The word "tutelage" is taken in its oldest sense (ca. 1650) as "the condition of being under protection or guardianship." (Oxford).

CHAPTER 4

STRUCTURE OF THE CODE OF ETHICS

. . . fairness . . . loyalty . . . fidelity . . . ideals of . . .
honour and . . . integrity.

Section 1 of the Code of Ethics comprises only fifty-seven
words—words that shine in the brilliant light of the concepts
represented by six abstract nouns, quoted above without context.
This section is the law and the prophets; to it the remaining sections stand as commentary. As in Lord Nelson's famous summary of the science of naval tactics—"no captain can go far
wrong who lays his ship alongside that of an enemy''—it is more
than a statement of duties; the inescapable inference tells us what
we are expected to be.

The weight given section 1 does not disparage the content of
sections 2 to 6, which derive from it. These are interpretations of
section 1 as it applies to various recurring situations in which it is
important that interpretation be uniform, so that members of the
profession may know what to expect of each other and the public
may know what to expect of members of the profession. Each
canon is set forth as an imperative; the steps of argument from
section 1 are not given. In terms of analogy, star azimuths give us
our ultimate standard for direction, but we steer by a compass of
characteristics established by reference to that standard.

Subscribing to the Code of Ethics, we accept these uniform
interpretations as mandatory in the circumstances to which they
apply. But there is an infinity of situations, and when we examine
the compass card we find that it is marked on its periphery for
only a few of them—the canons of sections 2 to 6, to escape the
analogy—and what we have to cope with may not be among   47

those indicated. We must lay a course for ourselves. The usual attack is to carry out a sort of interpolation between sets of circumstances dealt with in sections 2 to 6, and to submit the finding to the test of section 1. The latter step is essentially an examination of conscience; face to face with the uncompromising simplicity of section 1, your authors do not venture to expatiate. About the first step, there are things to be said, and writings to be quoted.

In another chapter of this book, typical examination questions in the subject Professional Practice and Ethics as given by APEO appear, and in yet another, some typical answers are given. It will be seen at once that the questions simulate practical situations about which candidates are asked to make decisions on ethical grounds, perhaps to make decisions subject to conditions or assumptions they express, or even to demur, explaining why the information is, in their opinion, inadequate. What is to be demonstrated is not knowledge of the Code of Ethics—indeed, it is customary for candidates to have a copy of it on their desks as they write—but a comprehension of it that will enable them to interpolate, or perhaps extrapolate, from what is written in the code, and to reasonably justify their conclusions. Writing to such questions does not preclude the citing of personal ethics (section 1, again!) if the candidates feel that their consciences affect or override some tentative decision that is logical under sections 2 to 6, but the examiners in past years have not encountered such conflicts. Certainly, no intent to set up traps of this nature has existed in the preparation of the question papers. Indeed, it is difficult to imagine complexities and delicacies that would enable such a conflict to be presented.

Situations posed in examination questions are necessarily described in few words. Candidates may bring in additional background and ancillary characters, stating any such assumptions, if they feel that these clarify the reasoning for their answers to the question; if such background has no such purpose, it is, of course, superfluous. It is adverse if it is a means of sidestepping the thrust of the question.

In the ''Manual of Professional Practice'' (APEO, 1982), section 7, entitled ''Rules of Practice'', is, in its own words, ''directed principally to the practical realities of operating a professional engineering business.'' Other aspects enter the treatment given, but the Code of Ethics is the overriding philosophy, and no equally good illustration of practical application of the canons involved is known to your authors. Parts of this valuable discussion are reproduced here with the permission of APEO, and indexed so that they may be keyed for reference either from the left (the nature of the ethical problem treated) or from the right (subsections of the Code of Ethics cited), as follows:

SUBSECTION OF

Rules of Practice	*Code of Ethics*
• Definition	
• Comparison with Rules of Professional Conduct	
• Practising Beyond One's Competence	6(b)
• Reviewing of Another Engineer's Work	5(a), (b)
• Conflict of Interest	2(a), (c); 3(a), (c), (d), (e), (f); 4(a), (b)
• Negligence	2(e), (f); 4(c)
• Competitive Bidding	5(f)
• Confidential Information	3(a)

RULES OF PRACTICE

Definition

Rules of Practice might be defined as a professionally acceptable series of guidelines designed to assist the practitioner in conducting a professional engineering practice with minimum risk of contravening ethical, business, or legal requirements on him.

Comparison with Rules of Professional Conduct

The Code of Ethics is a recitation of the moral principles which govern the personal conduct of the practising professional. The Code is not for the governance or the guidance of the client, the employer, or the business contact. It is a guide to the professional as to his personal conduct in relation to all of the parties involved. It is for their protection, not for his.

On the other hand, Rules of Practice are directed principally to the practical realities of operating a professional 49 engineering business. The emphasis is on the business aspects, although the principles of ethical conduct are connected therewith in many instances. Rules of Professional Practice are for the information and the protection of the practising professional; they will assist the individual in establishing and maintaining a reputation for sound business practices as well as for professional integrity.

Not only must engineering practice be beyond question as to its professional and business characteristics, it must be seen to be beyond question. Ensuring the latter often means the reinforcing of professional conduct principles by business or political realities, or vice versa. It is the interaction of the two precepts which provides the surest foundation for a successful practice.

There are numerous internal and external standards which must be observed meticulously in practice; there are numerous external regulations and statutes which impinge on engineering practice and on engineering businesses. These may be professional, municipal, provincial, federal or international in nature, depending on individual circumstances of practice. A few of the more common situations—and caveats—are outlined in the following sections.

Practising Beyond One's Competency

Without referring to related civil or criminal offences, the professional engineer must know that there are both legal and ethical compulsions on him in this respect. Failure to meet these requirements leaves a practitioner open to professional scrutiny, either informal or formal, by his professional association, and to penalties of various degrees up to and including cancellation of membership, should he be judged "guilty" by his peers.

The Code of Ethics provides the following requirement of the practitioner:

6(b) "A professional engineer shall undertake only such work as he is competent to perform by virtue of his training and experience, and shall, where advisable, retain and cooperate with other professional engineers or specialists."

The foregoing must surely be judged a commonsense exhortation by most engineers, who, when in any doubt, will seek the necessary support of those better qualified than are they themselves. Of course, there are bound to be borderline instances and, in such cases, the practitioner may be appropriately convinced of his own abilities. He must know that he may be required to defend his actions should problems arise. His defence can only be that he is in fact "competent . . . by virtue of his training and experience . . .". The inclusion of the two elements of competence provides the practitioner with the ability to maximize his qualifications.

Competence goes beyond the formal qualification of the engineer to practice. It has to do with the sufficiency of the engineer's qualifications to deal with the particular problem or circumstances at hand. It includes knowledge, experience, and skill, and the ability to use them effectively in the interest of the client or employer.

An engineer, therefore, should not undertake a matter unless he honestly believes that he is competent to proceed effectively, or that he can become competent without undue delay, risk or expense to his client or employer, or that he will engage a suitable "expert" or "specialist" in the areas in question. If an engineer proceeds on any other basis, he is not being honest with his client or employer. This is an ethical consideration, and must be distinguished from the standard of care that a court would require in dealing with negligence.

In the more formal professional sense, The Professional Engineers Act, Chapter 394, RSO 1980, describes in Section 25 the procedures by which the Council may act against a member alleged to be guilty of professional misconduct. For the purposes of such disciplinary procedures, professional misconduct is defined in the Regulations made under the Act. That definition includes:

Section 8(c) . . . Incompetence,

and in turn Section 9(b) further defines incompetence as:

"lack of adequate knowledge of, or continued neglect or failure to exercise the ordinary skills of a professional engineer".

As has been mentioned previously, the professional tribunal may not demand "perfection" of the engineer. It may, and ordinarily will, establish what standard of competence is acceptable in the particular instance, by eliciting from senior engineers of prominence and reputation, or of other special qualifications, what practices are in fact carried on

51

by professionals in general, and what qualities or standards the industry considers acceptable in order to ensure the well being of the public. The defence to such a charge to be successful must demonstrate that the practice or standard of a significant segment of the profession in related circumstances, is of no higher quality than that delivered by the defendant.

There may well be tendencies to accentuate the charge by reference to "negligence." This, however, is a separate matter and must be suitably incorporated into the formal charge as such, and dealt with independently. A latter section will deal with "gross negligence."

"Incompetence" is not an uncommon charge against members of APEO. As many as twelve cases in one year have been considered by Council or its Disciplinary Committee, with the direction that the decision be published in the Official Journal of the Association.

Reviewing of Another Engineer's Work

This is a "problem" which has both ethical and practical business elements. It is one which arises frequently, and which often causes undue outbursts of emotions, based largely on the individual engineer's often incomplete or erroneous understanding of professional ethics, or business practice, or of common courtesies.

The Code of Ethics references are:

5(a) "A professional engineer shall conduct himself towards other professional engineers with courtesy and good faith.

5(b) A professional engineer shall not accept any engagement to review the work of another professional engineer for the same employer except with the knowledge of that engineer, or except where the connection of that engineer with the work has been terminated."

From the foregoing, it is clear that an engineer's ethical obligation is discharged adequately, if he simply informs the first engineer with due courtesy that he has been approached. He is then free to make his own decision. In the normal course of events, the act of courtesy in "informing" the first engineer of the approach to him also provides an opportunity to discuss the project, and to understand not only the first engineer's position, but to gain a better or at least another view of the owner's objectives. With these "common-sense" background data, the second engineer can make his decision, in fairness to all three parties involved, if possible, but at least with professional and business requirements satisfied reasonably. The ethical exhortation, therefore, can be met with a simple discloser of approach; courtesy and common sense suggest that the communication between the two individual engineers can also be "good business."

The most frequent misconception engineers seem to have is found in both engineers involved. Engineer No. 1 often believes that engineer No. 2 must have his permission to engage in a review of his work; engineer No. 2 often believes he should not proceed without that permission. As seen from the foregoing, the seeking or granting of permission is *not* an ethical requirement. Should either party wish to make it a condition of proceeding then it must be embodied as a specific requirement in any contractual documents signed by the various parties involved.

Another misconception found frequently is that the original engineer cannot be said to have been "terminated" unless and until his "fees" owing have been duly and fully paid. This is not the case; termination involves written notice, in accordance with the terms of the contract between the parties, if such exists. "Cancellation" or termination claims of the dismissed engineer are thenceforward a contractual matter between the two, to be resolved through legal proceedings if necessary, or a claim in tort for damages, also subject to resolution by means of legal proceedings.

Review of one engineer's work by another is a "normal" procedure in everyday engineering. In all employment situations there are specified checks, balances, and reviews designed not only to ensure technical competence, but to ensure compliance with specifications, to ensure compatibility with other components, systems, equipment or manufacturing processes, to ensure environmental, economic, and even business and political climates will not be offended. Most engineers understand and accept these realities.

However, if one does the original engineer the courtesy of telling him of the approach which has been made, and

53

one listens to what he has to say, one will not only be acting in accordance with professional ethical requirements, but will be using good business sense.

Conflict of Interest

Of all of the ethical exhortations on the practising professional, that most frequently referred to by the Code is "Conflict of Interest." In fact, the references are numerous, and generally clear. They are as follows:

2(a) "A professional engineer shall regard his duty to the public welfare as paramount."

2(c) "A professional engineer shall not give opinions or make statements on professional engineering projects of public interest that are inspired or paid for by private interests unless he clearly discloses on whose behalf he is giving the opinions or making the statements."

3(a) "A professional engineer shall act in professional engineering matters for each employer as a faithful agent or trustee and shall regard as confidential any information obtained by him as to business affairs, technical methods or processes of an employer and avoid or disclose any conflict of interest which might influence his actions or judgement."

3(c) "A professional engineer shall have no interest, direct or indirect, in any materials, supplies or equipment used by his employer or any persons or firms receiving contracts from his employer unless he informs his employer in advance of the nature of the interest."

3(d) "A professional engineer shall not tender on competitive work upon which he may be acting as a professional engineer unless he first advises his employer."

3(e) "A professional engineer shall not act as a consulting engineer in respect of any work upon which he may be the contractor unless he first advises his employer."

3(f) "A professional engineer shall not accept compensation, financial or otherwise, for a particular service, from more than one person, except with the full knowledge of all interested parties."

4(a) "A professional engineer in private practice . . . shall disclose immediately any interest, direct or indirect, which might in any way be construed as prejudicial to his professional judgement in rendering service to his client;'' and

4(b) "If he is an employee-engineer and is contracting in his own name to perform professional engineering work for other than his employer, shall provide his client with a written statement of the nature of his status as an employee and the attendant limitations on his services to the client. In addition he shall satisfy himself that such work will not conflict with his duty to his employer.''

The foregoing listing simply illustrates the many situations in which a professional engineer may find himself and which can involve "conflict of interest." There is, then, a tremendous potential for "conflict of interest" situations in the day-to-day business of engineering. Excepting 2(a) above, it will be seen that the letter of the ethical exhortation would seem to be met if the engineer involved is simply careful to divulge to all parties directly involved his precise position. In other words, disclosure alone would satisfy the Code of Ethics.

However, while it may be relatively simple to "disclose" pertinent matters to parties of the first part and to parties of the second part, adequate disclosure to affected third parties—the public welfare, as noted in 2(a)—is much more difficult. If the engineer is to avoid conflict of interest situations, he must also avoid the appearance of conflict; his reputation and credibility may well be more dependent on the latter than on the former.

The professional engineer will then:

(i) avoid involvement in conflict of interest situations wherever possible;

(ii) if the situation cannot be avoided, ensure that full disclosure to the affected parties is made prior to his involvement;

(iii) take especial pains to see that a conflict of interest cannot be perceived to exist by third parties, the affected public; it's not only good ethics, it's good business!

Negligence

"Negligence" is closely related to "incompetence," but is usually characterized by such words as "carelessness,"   55 "disregard," "indifference." The Code of Ethics makes no direct reference to "negligence" but, by implication, it can be seen that failure to comply with the requirements of Sections 2(e), 2(f) and 4(c) would normally be considered to be "negligence" in some degree. The Sections involved are:

2(e) "A professional engineer shall make effective provisions for the safety and health of a person who may be affected by the work for which he is responsible; and at all times shall act to correct or report any situation which he feels may endanger the safety or the welfare of the public."

2(f) "A professional engineer shall make effective provision for meeting lawful standards, rules, or regulations relating to environmental control and protection, in connection with any work being undertaken by him or under his responsibility."

4(c) "A professional engineer shall carry out his work in accordance with applicable statutes, regulations, standards, codes, and by-laws."

In a statutory sense, engineers must look to Regulation 802, Sections 8 and 9, to understand the authority and the obligation of the Association in respect of "negligence." Section 8(a) refers to one aspect of professional misconduct as "gross negligence." Section 9(a) states "gross negligence" means "an act or omission in the carrying out of work of a professional engineer that shows a reckless or deliberate disregard of or indifference to the rights and safety of others."

It has been the custom of the Association to consider individual minor and inadvertent omissions or carelessness, which do not bear directly on the safety of the public or of the integrity of the works themselves, as matters for informal review through Practice and Ethics Procedures. More serious or oft repeated omissions may be dealt with more formally as "incompetence" involving "failure to exercise. . . ."

However, when in the opinion of the Committee the facts of the case studied, show repeated or major omissions, which in turn could result from "deliberate" or "reckless" actions or omissions on the part of the engineer, and which would jeopardize the safety of the works themselves, or of those affected thereby in any way, then formal charges of "gross negligence" will be recommended. Civil or criminal charges of negligence against a professional engineer could be expected to "trigger" corresponding professional charges.

Professional engineers must be particularly careful to understand their obligations for compliance with a mass of "external" regulations and statutes bearing on the public welfare and safety. Examples might well include The Ontario Building Code, The Industrial Safety Act, The Construction Safety Act, Electrical Codes; there are many others. In hearings relative to "gross negligence" or "incompetence," their individual actions may well be measured against these "external" requirements.

Competitive Bidding

Of concern to engineers in private practice is an increasing tendency of public bodies to seek professional services through competitive bidding procedures. Numerous American engineering and other professional codes of ethics have contained prohibitions against the practice. However, these have been challenged under U.S. anti-trust legislation and, as a result, have been withdrawn by the parties involved. The principal organizations bowing to the anti-trust decrees are the American Society of Civil Engineers, the American Institute of Architects, the American Institute of Public Accountants, and the National Society of Professional Engineers. The essence of findings of the U.S. Supreme Court is contained in the words "no ethical rule which is anti-competitive may survive."

It is necessary to dispel the belief that in Canada and in Ontario competitive bidding for professional services is illegal or at least unethical. There are no laws forbidding the practice; there are no ethical rules prohibiting its use. Examination of APEO's Code of Ethics will disclose no reference to competitive bidding. It is well to understand that Canada's Combines Investigations Act is structured after the Sherman Act of USA and, as a consequence, no engineering organization, for instance, may attempt to prevent its members from engaging in competitive bidding practices.

The foregoing does not in itself establish any particular sympathy for the practice among professionals. Indeed, APEO has long felt that competitive bidding is a singularly inappropriate method for the selection of professionals, and has recommended selection procedures which rely on qualifications and performance. This preference is referred to in APEO Fee Schedules and Performance Standards in the section on "Recommended Procedure for the Selection of an Engineer to Provide Professional Services."

Faced with a request to provide competitive pricing for professional services, the engineer is left to his own judgement. There being no professional prohibition of the practice, he is free to comply if he so desires, or to avoid making a proposal (with whatever consequences that may have) if he feels strongly that it is not proper or suitable for him to do so.

Confidential Information

Section 3(a) of the Code of Ethics makes specific reference to confidentiality, amongst other things, as follows:

3(a) "A professional engineer shall act in professional engineering matters for each employer as a faithful agent or trustee, and *shall regard as confidential any information obtained by him as to the business affairs, technical methods or processes of an employer* and avoid or disclose any conflict of interest which might influence his actions or judgement."

From the foregoing, it is clear that a professional engineer may not divulge any such information to third parties unless he is expressly or implicitly authorized by his client, or employer, or is required by law to do so. Unreserved communication between practitioner and client or employer is essential to effective delivery of professional services. The client or employer must feel completely secure and he is entitled to assume this to be the case without any request on his part as to the maintenance of confidentiality. He is similarly entitled to assume that the duty of confidentiality will survive the professional commission which required it, and that it will continue indefinitely after termination of contracts or relationships.

A professional engineer is expected to avoid the disclosure of such information and to avoid the use thereof for the benefit of himself or a third party, or to the disadvantage of his employer or client. He would be expected to decline employment or commission which would require him to make such disclosures.

Employed engineers may be concerned as to the precise obligation upon them when changing employment within their field. It is generally considered that an engineer may apply in his new position any information or expertise gained by him in the old position, as long as it falls into a "state of the art" category which has become general knowledge through publication to the profession. However, he is not entitled to apply in his new position information gained in the old position which is of a proprietary nature, and which is considered to fall into the category of "Trade Secrets."

In the preparation of material for technical publications, an engineer will be particularly careful to avoid inadvertent disclosure of confidential information, and will seek approval or consent of the affected parties before submitting such information for publication.

The exhortation of the Code of Ethics would appear to prevent a professional engineer from engaging in the now popular practice of "leaking" confidential information of his employer to adversary parties, or to the public press.

However, because an engineer's duty to the public welfare is paramount (Section 2[a] of the Code of Ethics) he may be required in certain situations to make disclosures where public safety is involved. There is a basic difference between the "leaking" process, and the "disclosure" process the engineer may be compelled to follow. The former is essentially furtive, anonymous and selfish, with objectives of revenge or embarrassment to a person or a party; the latter is open, very personal, and conducted with the interest of the public in mind. The engineer puts his name on the action and his job on the line.

The procedure to be followed by the professional engineer begins with the instruction of Section 3(b) of the Code of Ethics which states "a professional engineer shall present clearly to his employers the consequences to be expected from any deviations proposed in the work if his professional engineering judgement is overruled by non-technical authority in cases where he is responsible for the technical adequacy of professional engineering work." Should he not receive satisfaction from his immediate superior, he should pursue his concerns with higher authorities within his organization. Failing satisfaction internally, he should then present his concerns to the appropriate public authority. Similarly, in accordance with the exhortation of Section 2(e) he shall "act at all times to correct or report any situation which he feels may endanger the safety or welfare of the public," following a similar "path," depending on circumstances.

ETHICAL VS. LEGAL REQUIREMENTS

In any situation, there could be a difference between the ethical obligations and legal requirements of the professional engineer.

> The regulatory authorities that govern engineering in the province have established specific standards of conduct; the code of ethics details those standards. Those standards are not necessarily synonymous with the standard of care expected of the engineer according to the common law. For example, particular conduct may result in disciplinary sanctions against an engineer pursuant to the Code of Ethics but liability at common law may not necessarily arise.
>
> Marston, *Law for Professional Engineers*
> (McGraw-Hill Ryerson, 1981)

The foregoing suggests an excellent exercise in the process of achieving comprehension, as distinct from knowledge, of the Code of Ethics. With respect, your authors suggest that the first sentence could well have been extended by adding the words "as applied to frequently recurring circumstances."

In a thoughtful contemplation of each item of sections and subsections 2 to 6, the student might ask:

a. Can I connect this item with what is said in section 1 and illustrate the connection in a dozen words or less?

b. Can I imagine a set of circumstances in which an offence against this item of the code of ethics would also involve "liability at common law"? To answer this, one does not have to cite any law; only the degree of familiarity with law normally possessed by the educated person is necessary. For instance, subsection 2b, binding as it is in ethics, does not seem likely to give rise to "liability at common law," while contravention of item 5c might well do so. Very few words should suffice here; Darwin is reputed to have said that what he could not explain of his work to the cook in a few minutes he probably did not understand himself!

c. Have I checked to see whether reference is made to this item in the APEO Rules of Practice given in the preceding paragraph? This may affect the answer, and in any case it will amplify perception of the significance of the item.

d. Do I realize that the penalty for transgression of the Code of Ethics, P.E. Act 25(1)1, may well be more severe and damaging to my career than a finding against me of "liability at common law"? In the former, even an outcome of unwarranted proceedings, P.E. Act 25(1)6, an exoneration, should lead us to reflect with the poet:

> . . . it is well if the Court shall acquit thee,
> It were best had'st thou never been tried.
> Hopwood, "The Laws of the Navy"

CHAPTER 5

THE ENGINEER AS VICAR

Vicar: one who takes the place of or acts instead of
another.

The Oxford Universal Dictionary

There is an obvious similarity between the role and duty of an
employee engineer as a faithful agent or trustee of the employer
and the role and duty of a consulting engineer as an adviser to
and, at times, agent of the client in professional engineering matters. Employees' roles are not always as clearly defined as that of
the consultant because so much of their work is in-house; in their
engineering they are faithful agents, not only of the employer,
but of their fellow employees also, whose safety, comfort, productivity and general welfare are affected by the engineers' exercise of ingenuity, their design decisions and their care that the
decisions are carried out. In dealing with other than fellow
employees their position is similar to that of the consulting engineer. In both cases the engineers are in a position where they are
the visible presence of the owner in the direction and control of a
project as it is carried through its different stages by the contractor. By substituting ''master mechanic'' or ''production superintendent'' for ''contractor'' and thinking of the mill or factory as
the site, we envisage the similarity in the philosophy of those
relationships, be it factory or site work.

Hugh Adcock, P.Eng. (a former councillor of APEO and
recently retired as assistant deputy minister, Ministry of Transportation and Communications, province of Ontario) has contri-
buted the following thoughts, comments, advice and suggested
guidelines for the field engineer in the art of combining tact with

ethical conduct in the sometimes delicate task of field engineering, under the heading Engineer-Contractor Relationships:

> One of the more difficult problems the field engineer has to face is his personal relations with the contractor when he is the engineer-in-charge of a project. It is very hard to strike just the right note in personal relations. Some men are born with this "knack of leadership." They never have to argue. They never raise their voices. They say "do this" and it's done. They have the respect of their associates and run a job well. Conversely, some engineers do not have this knack and never learn it. They find it very hard to get contractors to obey instructions. They are either too easy-going or too rigid. The result is constant bickering and lack of harmony. The job and the owner suffer.
>
> Just what should be the attitude of the engineer toward the contractor? How can a balanced, harmonious relationship be attained—and maintained?
>
> There are no hard-and-fast rules. Individuals vary, as do jobs and contractors. The contractor is in business to make money. The engineer's task is to see that the job gets done and done right. These different viewpoints are not necessarily incompatible.
>
> It is well to realize, and it should not be too difficult to convince the contractor, that all job forces are on the same team. The owner wants the best job he is entitled to, at the earliest practicable time. The engineer and the inspectors are there to get this job done for the owner. But the engineer is also an arbiter and must resist any pressure on the contractor to do more than the contract calls for or to do extra work without fair compensation. You will find that most contractors want to build and maintain a reputation for good work.
>
> In the interest of better engineer-contractor relations and to help young engineers who are just starting in the profession to develop leadership, the following six points are worthy of your consideration.

BE FIRM

Once you have made up your mind, stick to it. Let's assume that you have thoroughly thought out a certain situation and have made a decision. You tell the contractor that something must be done in a certain manner. He starts raising the roof. Don't let him scare you. Nine times out of ten he is screaming for effect—or just to see how serious you really are. If you let his noise bother you, or change your mind, you are in for a lot of the same treatment every time. Make sure you are right. If you think you are, stick to it. But if some time you really are wrong, be man enough to admit it and correct your error. You will not lose standing by being fair.

DON'T LET ANYBODY RUSH YOU

Many times you may be asked for a quick decision. Don't be hurried. It's best to take the situation back to the office with you and think it over in all its ramifications. You can be sure that the other fellow has thought it over. Ask yourself if this change or decision you have to make affects only what you are doing now, or will affect something else later. Remember that you may be setting a precedent. Nothing looks quite so bad as changing your mind once you realize the full implications of your snap decision. You can't tell the contractor one thing one day and another thing the next.

BE FAIR

Many young engineers, and older ones too, have a tendency to apply specifications too rigidly. They "go by the book." Even when they are shown an equal or better solution to a problem, they insist on following the specifications to the letter. In situations like that, common sense is your best friend. Your judgment will tell you when your contractor is honestly trying to do a good job. Remember, many contractors have been around a good many years and have had a lot of experience. It pays to listen. There will be lots of times when you will be glad you did.

DON'T BE OVERFRIENDLY

Many contractors try to cultivate the engineer. They are very eager to please him and to become good friends. Starting with coffee breaks, you may go to lunch and have a drink, and before you know it you will wind up by being very, very chummy. You'll be on a first-name basis. Soon you'll start thinking that the contractor is a fairly good Joe. Quite probably he is a very pleasant fellow.

Now you are in something of a predicament. Because, when the situation comes up—and it surely must—it's awfully hard to tell one of your "friends" to do something you know very well he isn't going to like doing. You are going to be thrown together often during the course of your project. And no one wants you to be stiff and unfriendly. A pleasant, courteous attitude with a modicum of reserve will help maintain an easy businesslike relationship. However, you should not let friendliness distort your judgment and lead you into "friendly," biased, and unsound decisions. Keep your friends for your personal life.

THINK AHEAD

It is taken for granted that the engineer is thoroughly familiar with what is happening on his project every day. But how about what's going to happen tomorrow? Try to anticipate tomorrow's trouble today. Look ahead. If you spot any trouble, talk it over with the contractor. Your foresight will probably save money for both the owner and the contractor.

BE A DIPLOMAT

A soft answer gets better results than loud talk. Ask or suggest rather than order. Grease the wheels a little. An engineer acts somewhat as a broker in that he tries to bring both parties, owner and contractor, together in harmony, the end result being a job well done.

For better or for worse you are stuck with your contractor for the duration. It's a delicate situation at best. But with common sense and good engineer-contractor relationships, your owner will get a good job, your contractor will do all right, and you will increase your stature in your chosen profession.

In-house activities of the employee engineer generally involve long-term day-to-day relations with a relatively permanent group. What Hugh Adcock says applies to in-house relationships also; the employee engineer shares to some degree the interests of long-term fellow employees. Usually he cannot subscribe wholly to any group ethic—declared or perceived—among them. In the welter of labour laws that prevail across Canada and the U.S.— probably throughout the industrialized world—the engineer is not commonly included by compulsion in industrial unions but is identified with management. There are many instances, no doubt, where a union affiliation is required of engineers, particularly during early stages of learning the processes of an industry that involve periods of work at different jobs prior to engaging in the practice of professional engineering in these precincts. There is no prohibition of such affiliations in the Code of Ethics and it will probably be only in actively adversarial circumstances that young engineers will have to judge their conduct with nicety. To have to face such judgements is the price of maturity for every man and woman.

Professional unions exist in some large organizations where there are many employee professional engineers. These, presumably, are able to conduct negotiations concerning their interests with the employer without contravention of the Code of Ethics. Fairness and loyalty travel two-way streets, and a common interpretation of these virtues can be reached without grievous belligerence.

For employee engineers in public service and, with variations, in the armed forces, a patchwork pattern (federal, provincial, municipal) of what amount to contractual obligations, sometimes accepted under oath, may impinge marginally upon the Code of Ethics (as in the matter of secrecy versus Section 6[a] of the Code) but at the sophisticated level of practice at which such conflicts might appear, reconciliation of both obligations seems possible.

For further information on those special aspects of ethics that are related to professional engineering practice in public service, civil or military, your authors recommend the book *Ethical Conduct: Guidelines for Government Employees* by Kenneth Kernaghan. Published in 1975 by the Institute of Public Administration of Canada, the book presents an excellent treatment of the subject. In its foreword it is stated that "the Institute is specifically enjoined by its Constitution to concern itself with questions of public duty and professional etiquette."

The guideline deals with these questions in Canada in the federal, provincial and municipal governments and makes comparison with the nature and treatment of the problem in the central governments of Great Britain and the United States.

CHAPTER 6

PROFESSIONAL ENGINEERS IN THE MANUFACTURING INDUSTRY

While the engine runs, the people must work; men,
women and children are yoked together with iron and
steam. The animal machine is chained to the iron machine
that knows no sickness and no weariness.
  Hammond and Hammond, *The Rise of Modern Industry*

This bitter passage is quoted by the Hammonds from writing of
the late 1700s, that darkest period of the Industrial Revolution
that followed the adaptation of the engine to the driving of rotat-
ing shafts, the "fateful combination of fire and the wheel" by
which our technological society was born, and of which the mis-
ery and sorrow were only gradually abated in the ensuing half-
century.

Watt died in 1819 in his eighty-third year. There is a portrait
statue of him in Westminster Abbey, inscribed:

JAMES WATT
who, directing the forces of an original genius,
early exercised in philosophic research,
to the improvement of
THE STEAM ENGINE,
enlarged the resources of his country,
increased the power of Man,
and rose to an eminent place among the most
illustrious followers of science and the real
benefactors of the world.

For generations these two conflicting philosophies have exercised moralists in our society. At what level of immediate threat to the welfare of the human race shall engineers and scientists stay their hands? And if they do so, to what extent may they be failing to become "real benefactors of the world"? Yet, in practical life, the questions have a certain unreality. Given human nature, neither discovery nor development will be locked away in the hope that some era of perfected humanity will arrive. In one of the scenes of a play concerned with such speculations, God is told that people from Planet Earth had landed on the Moon. "Ah yes", He said, "I was there. It was most gratifying. Man has been so slow to learn about the world I put him in charge of. After all this time he's beginning to realize what he can do with the tools I have given him."

The foot of humankind is set on an irreversible path, and if we have traded off something of the immemorial concepts that gave dignity and stability to the individual, accepting in return a philosophy of endless economic growth and endless increase in the material standard of living, we can only strive to organize our world so that we may exist in reasonable harmony with our destiny. Having all but forgotten fear of God, we must learn to meet the new fears that beset us.

CANADIAN TECHNOLOGY IN MANUFACTURING

Canadians live under the psychological dominance of the United States. We want their "standard of living," indeed, feel we deserve it in spite of obviously different circumstances. To do so, we have to import most products and much production technology; we simply cannot afford to do it ourselves because our market is too small. The cancellation of the Avro Arrow in the late 1950s brought this crushing reality into focus. Less obvious is the foreign or government ownership of much of our large manufacturing industry such as aircraft, automobile and appliance. We do not lack the ability (the Arrow was potentially great) or the desire; we just cannot afford it.

Despite this, Canada poses some unique problems of climate, geography and culture that other countries do not have to the same degree. In these areas, our technology has flourished and we are able to export this to fill the weaker needs of foreign countries. In 'bush' aircraft, snow-removal equipment, railway products, snowmobiles, bridges, large-scale farm equipment, Canada is a leader in both design and manufacture.

New generations of youthful engineers and keen immigrants from foreign lands are adding a new impetus that will bring fresh vigor to Canada. The important thing is that we exercise wisdom and restraint to attack appropriate problems with appropriate engineering.

THE ROLE OF THE PROFESSIONAL ENGINEER

We are fortunate that engineering is a recognized profession in Canada, unlike many other countries, and professional engineers are in a powerful and responsible position in our technological society. Eighty-five percent of them are a part of large organizations, most generally manufacturing establishments. Their established ethics, as members of a profession, is valuable security to any employer. The same code that establishes the long-range goals of the professional engineer is either complementary to or the same as the employer's. As a result, engineers are in the most diversified and far-flung of all the professions and at least half work in jobs with no relation to design at all. The only other profession approaching this situation is accounting.

Let us now examine the role of professional engineers in this picture. Obviously they have a major part to play in nearly every aspect. Less obvious is the fact that they have a greatly different relationship to their employer than do their colleagues in private practice. Private practitioners enter into a three-way enterprise to provide service, together with the owner of the work and contractor who will build it. The owner and professional engineer have one contract, the owner and contractor a separate contract. Thus the engineer in private practice serves the interest of the owner. On the other hand, the employee engineer is in the service of the "contractor" or manufacturer and seldom has any relation at all to the "owner" or purchaser of the product. By the principle of vicarious liability, the employer is liable for the negligent acts of employees; thus the responsibility of professional engineers as employees is to protect the employer, rather than the owner, from harm. The end result is the same, yet the employee engineer may have an even greater responsibility in the sense that manufactured goods are produced in such large quantity and manufacturers have not only substantial wealth, but a great concern for their corporate responsibility, and are particularly vulnerable to immense liability lawsuits. This is applicable also to the process of manufacturing where similar crushing liability suits arise over safety, environmental and social issues. In all this the need for powerful, proven ethical standards is evident; the already proven ethics of the engineer is a near perfect match to the need.

PRODUCT

This is the classic work of engineers. Although the concept may or may not be theirs, they are responsible for the efficient, adequate design and for definition of the loads, performance and safety requirements. They carry out the scientific task of calculating performance and strength, proving the product prototype in shop tests and later field tests and repeating each step by iteration until optimization is achieved. This process involves a continuing participation in improving input design parameters (with users, specifying bodies, and so on) and in matching the design to the most efficient available production processes. It also involves working with other manufacturers and agencies, such as standards organizations, since a new development is seldom carried by one firm.

The product function is very broad and encompasses the entire life-cycle from research and development, through initial production, continued improvement over its life and responsibility for quality control, reliability and field servicing. The mature firm handles this through a series of departments such as research and development, product engineering, test department, quality assurance and customer service. Typically, professional engineers are employed to carry out and/or supervise and manage the work of all aspects.

MANUFACTURING

The design and construction of the industrial process is the task of the industrial engineer, as is the continued improvement that is so imperative in a competitive nation. Similarly, selecting the manufacturing process and designing the tools for producing new products and components is a part of this task. An offshoot of this, of crucial importance, is the procurement of materials and complex planning of schedules to assure an efficient and orderly flow of materials into and out of the factory. A second offshoot is the responsibility for safety within the plant and protection of the environment from pollutants created in the process. The maintenance of the equipment in efficient working order affects almost all aspects and is a further major responsibility.

Traditionally, the leadership of manufacturing is generated from its own ranks, and this is still frequently the case even in large organizations. However, the increasing complexity of the production process and the enormous cost of larger installations has seen a trend toward the engagement of professional engineers, particularly at levels of supervisory responsibility. A large part of this is due to increasing technical complexity of the equipment. The broad educational base of engineers gives them not only a basic understanding; they are also equipped with a methodology (the "scientific method") to tackle new and abstract problems that the shop worker does not have. Since future corporate management will be formed from these ranks in many cases, the trend toward hiring engineers is continuing, and accounts for a large part of the fifty percent of engineers whose work has little conventional engineering content.

MARKETING

Without sales of its products, the company cannot exist. Usually professional engineers have nothing at all to do with sales of consumer goods, but they have much to do with the rational sale of technical products, particularly where the 'customer' is another engineer or technologist. In general the more complex the product and its application, the greater the involvement of the engineer in its promotion. Marketing includes direct sales, advertising, application studies, negotiation of contracts and preparation of proposals (plus the occasional lunch). It may also include establishment, training and servicing of distribution networks. "Sales engineering" is another promotional tool, and a good one, in which engineering service is provided by a product manufacturer to assist customer-product engineers in using the product effectively and to inform them of the capabilities of a product.

No two organizations are constituted in the same manner. This is not only because of their different products and position in the life-cycle of their product; it also represents their "corporate strategy," the philosophy of management and the owners. Profound influences also are imposed by geography, social values, government policy and the labour force available. Therefore, one does not find the divisions clearly established, nor is the employment definition of the professional engineer predictable. 71

Further confusion is frequently added by the tendency of manufacturers to apply the title "engineer" to employees who lack professional status. These people, often shop trained and often competent in a narrow field of endeavour, are employed in engineering positions by their company, without professional status, in all facets up to and including product design. This situation is really a liability employers take on themselves. It is only of concern to the profession if such individuals carry the title engineer into the public arenas since the public is unable to discriminate between "engineer" and "professional engineer."

THE IMPORTANCE OF ETHICS
IN MANUFACTURING

Obviously, professional engineers in manufacturing are in a dynamic, evolving milieu as the corporate form continues to reshape under so many influences. The notable aspects are that more and more positions are being offered, the status of the employee engineers is rising markedly and their responsibilities are spreading horizontally and vertically throughout. This in turn is affecting both the concept of the profession itself and the nature of the engineer's education, which is being pressured toward more management training as well as technology.

It is likely that most employers are either unaware or only vaguely aware of the professional engineer's code of ethics. This indicates that the engineers themselves, through their image and behaviour, are earning the respect that is elevating their status and demand. The prime importance of the code of ethics therefore is the effect it has in shaping the attitude of engineers towards themselves and their colleagues.

An understanding of history will provide engineers with respect for their forebears and a strong respect for all other trades and professions. There is no reward in industry for arrogance. This same historical perspective will explain many questions regarding the status of the employee engineer in Canada. Above all it sets a challenge for our future, and the future of Canada.

When professional engineers, through training, experience, and by projecting the dignity inherent in their profession and ethics, have demonstrated their potential to contribute to the manufacturing community, they and their colleagues in that group will receive the same level of respect as is afforded the private practitioner. Public response will follow; indeed this is now clearly happening.

CHAPTER 7

STANDARDS AND CERTIFICATION

A unit is a particular amount of the physical quantity to be measured, defined in terms of a standard.
U.S. Bureau of Standards, Circular No. 60,1920

Standards for physical quantities do not normally give the scientist and the engineer much concern; to them, litre and gallon are volumes expressed in the dimension L, and if the units of L are in terms of the length of a metal bar cherished under glass, or of some fraction of the circumference of a great circle of a perfect terrestrial sphere, or of the wavelength of the electromagnetic radiation arising from the optical transition (in the orange range) in the isotope of krypton of mass 86, so be it.

Engineering design would be primitive without recognized standards for physical quantities. Our forefathers invented standards from time to time, or adapted existing standards. For example, the working capacity of a London draft horse was eventually expressed in terms of existing standards of force, length and time by Watt to give us a standard for power from which we derive nowadays kw, k cal/h, and so on by simple arithmetic, the draft horse having been relegated to history, except for his place in the word "horse-power." Today, it is only when we steer into distant and untravelled seas of scientific knowledge that a new basic standard is needed.

Arbitrarily calling a basic standard one that can be divided into units of quantity, one might propose a thesis that standards of quality or suitability in materials, functions of systems, workmanship, perhaps even beauty, could, in some ultimate analysis, be measured by evaluating a series of constituent standards of quantity by test. Such a thesis probably could not be sustained:

go/no-go tests (ultimately, it works/does not work) do not yield measures. In our context the speculation is idle, for it does not illustrate the important connection between established standards and the ethics of design. For this, let us look at 6(b) of the Code of Ethics:

> A professional engineer shall undertake only such work as he is competent to perform by virtue of his training and experience, and shall, where advisable, retain and co-operate with other professional engineers or specialists.

Seldom would a design project be entirely within the competence of one engineer or a group of engineers if there were not available a multitude of existing designs for components and subsystems of which the performance and suitability is guaranteed by others; the designer's competence under the code of ethics now lies in the training and experience by which the designer judges the knowledge and authority of those who give such a guarantee. Machine designers, for all their expertise, may not be really at home with electrical connections, but they do not have to retain an electrical engineer to specify the plug that will mate with domestic wall sockets. Their conscience and their legal obligations are satisfied because they accept the recommendation of a certifying body of recognized ability and integrity and so specify the component. They are accepting a standard of quality and suitability; in this example, a fitting about the size of a walnut, familiar to every homeowner, has been given minute study already; our machine designers need lose no sleep over it.

The International Organization for Standardization (ISO) defines a standard as:

> A technical specification or other document available to the public, drawn up with the co-operation and consensus or general approval of all interests affected by it, based on the consolidated results of science, technology and experience, aimed at the promotion of optimum community benefits and approved by a body recognized on the national, regional or international level.

The complexity of standards of quality is not always appreciated by the public for whose protection the standards have been defined; the indignant shopper who protests the difficulty arising from the advent of *ml* instead of *fl. oz.* is likely to find the labelling of a can of peas as *Canada Grade A* perfectly straightforward—a good example of our human propensity for straining at the gnat and swallowing the camel.

Certainly, standards that deal with materials, products, structures and systems are complex and time-sensitive; they are subject to frequent change to keep up with our fast-moving technology, environmental concerns and the future availability of materials. This is the type of standard that is the preoccupation of standards-writing organizations around the world.

However, in its simplest form a standard is no more and no less than a way to deal with a problem, a problem then can recur and if left unresolved can cause waste, unsafe conditions and dissatisfaction. The degree to which the standard solves the problem depends on the ability of those working on it to satisfy the various parties who may be affected. The formalizing of the process in a set of rules leads to the publication of a formal standard.

In Canada the need for formal standards arose during the First World War when a group of Canadian engineers and industrialists realized that if Canada were to progress as an industrial nation it needed formal engineering standards. The lack of such standards had, in many instances, seriously hindered the war effort.

Application was made to the federal government for a charter to establish an organization to develop national standards for Canada. The result was the creation, in 1919, of a voluntary nonprofit organization known as the Canadian Engineering Standards Association. Since then this organization has extended its activities well beyond the engineering field; in 1944 the name was changed to what it is today—the more appropriate Canadian Standards Association, or CSA. Other standards-writing organizations have also come into existence in Canada to serve specific needs.

Here is a partial list of American, Canadian and International Standards organizations whose activities affect Canadian practising engineers in many ways:

> American National Standards Institute (ANSI)
> American Society for Testing and Materials (ASTM)
> Bureau de Normalization du Quebec (BNQ)
> Canadian Gas Association (CGA)
> Canadian General Standards Board (CGSB)

Canadian Standards Association (CSA)
Institute of Electrical and Electronics Engineers (IEEE)
International Organization for Standardization (ISO)
Society of Automotive Engineers (SAE)
Underwriters' Laboratories of Canada (ULC).

We can scarcely imagine engineering design and procurement without their standards, either in domestic practice or in international commerce.

STANDARDS-WRITING IN CANADA

Because it is such a costly operation to develop a standard, careful consideration is given to ensure that there is truly a national need. However, once a decision to go ahead is made, the next step is to ensure that a properly constituted committee is established, one that is representative of all interests that may be affected by the standard; designers, manufacturers, purchasers, regulatory authorities, users and technical experts all become part of the process. In establishing the matrix of each committee, we try to provide a balance of interests so that no one individual group can unduly influence the process.

Another feature of Canadian standards development is that normally it is done on a two-tier basis—the technical committee responsible reports to an overview committee, which has the responsibility to ensure that the final document will not conflict with already published standards for similar or allied equipment and that proper steps have been taken and proper procedures observed, particularly with respect to the handling of negative comments.

In the development of a national standard under the Canadian system the consensus principle is used. That is to say, decisions are made through the reconciliation of diverse opinions until substantial, but not necessarily unanimous, agreement is reached within the standards committee.

To ensure that maximum use is made of what already exists, when starting a new project most committees will first look towards the international scene to see if a document is already available that may be adopted in its entirety or in part as the basis for the Canadian standard. Usually when an international standard is not available or is not suitable, we tend to look south of the border to our American friends because of the existing linkage between our two economies. The process is not always a one-way street: our counterparts in the U.S. often, in starting their standards projects, look to see what has been developed in Canada. In fact, there is effective liaison among standards organizations throughout the world and especially between those in the U.S. and Canada.

Because we are working under the principle of consensus, not everyone will be satisfied with the end product, and often to reach a satisfactory conclusion, trade-offs are necessary. This can sometimes present concerns to engineers, particularly when we consider that under the Code of Ethics professional engineers must regard their duty to public welfare as paramount. In some cases, the most stringent standard may not be the best one, particularly when we take into account a cost-benefit analysis or how the product might be used. For example, when the standard for hockey helmets was developed a few years ago, it was recognized that in order to be useful the standard had to allow for the production of a helmet that would be attractive and comfortable to the user as well as being relatively inexpensive so that it would be used by the majority of people involved in hockey. Yet at the same time, it had to protect the user and provide a reasonable degree of safety. The question of what is reasonable as opposed to what might be the ultimate can produce many hours of debate. There can be no easy set of guidelines to determine what is reasonable and each case must be examined on its own merits. In the case of the hockey helmet, the standard did its job and the product that is now being produced to the standard has all but eliminated certain injuries previously reported.

Engineers may also be put into a difficult position if they are in serious disagreement with other engineers on a committee. This problem can be compounded if, at a later date, the disagreeing engineers are asked to design or build in accordance with that standard after it has been published. A similar situation arises when engineers realize that their votes on a committee in favour of a particular standard may make the designs or products produced by the employer obsolete. Even if they are not made obsolete, added costs and changes may be such that the employer is placed in a situation where there is temporary or even long-term loss of market. Again, there are no easy answers.

Some comfort may be taken in the knowledge that standards-writing technical committees are made up, in large part, of professional engineers who are undoubtedly wrestling with the same matter of reconciling their decisions with the Code of Ethics. In any event, the committee member has to be satisfied that there has been no negligence in reaching a conclusion and that all points of view have been considered. It should be remembered that where an issue is controversial, there is often no right or wrong position; it is merely that there is more than one opinion as to the optimum.

In Canada today, the largest single group active in the development of standards is the engineers; probably this is true also for most of our trading partners, depending on what is accepted as the legal definition of an engineer in the country being considered. Within all of the Canadian standards-writing organizations (SWOs) there are close to ten thousand individuals involved in the standards development process and about three thousand of them are professional engineers. When we consider the direct costs borne by the various SWOs as well as the indirect costs paid by individual companies, government agencies and associations who pay the salaries and travel costs of those who attend standards meetings, a fair estimate of annual cost in Canada is more than a hundred million dollars. This business of standards is indeed big business with a pronounced engineering accent.

CERTIFICATION

In recent years, the idea of "certification" has gained prominence in the standards world. The concept, however, is not new; in fact, it had its origin in the very foundation of standardization. The first time a craftsman claimed that a product met a commonly accepted standard, the most basic form of certification came into being. Hallmarking, the listing or approval of products, the granting of the use of registered marks or certificates to indicate conformity to a standard, are all included in the general concept of certification. Changes in social and economic conditions have caused continuing evolution and growth of the certification process.

The costly procedure of developing a standard is futile unless that standard is used. It may be used in any of several ways. In many cases, designers and manufacturers voluntarily agree to follow appropriate standards and their customers accept their word. Here we are looking at a two-party system; the bulk of world trade is carried out on this basis. The customer or second party can, if it wishes, carry out its own audit of what is being produced but still only two individual groups are involved: the producer and the user. Over the years, however, business and trading patterns have become very complex. Quite often the end user has little knowledge of the producer and may wish to involve an independent or third party in the trading process, to act on behalf of the user to ensure that there is compliance with whatever standard is being used. This form of compliance with standards has now become universally known as third-party certification.

In many countries, and this is particularly true in North America, not only do purchasers require independent audits of manufacturers, but governments do also, especially when public health and safety are involved. For example, nearly all provinces in Canada now require that electrical products sold and/or installed within their respective boundaries must bear the CSA certification mark for their sale to be legal and for their installation to be approved. Similar regulations apply for fuel-burning appliances and other products.

In Canada, three of the major standards-writing organizations—CSA, CGA and ULC—offer certification services to their standards. Also, these three organizations provide certification services to other standards within their respective scope of activities. CGSB announced recently that it also intends to offer a certification service to its standards. Because of the close relationship between standards and certification, the Standards Council of Canada now accredits certification organizations, and it recently gave formal recognition to Warnock-Hersey Professional Services Ltd., which is not a standards-writing organization, but has for many years provided certification services in some of the same area of activities as Underwriters' Laboratories of Canada.

Although certification programs do vary from product to product, there are certain similar features regardless of which organization provides the service. Samples are usually required for test and evaluation, and a procedure that has come into use recently requires manufacturers to demonstrate how they intend to ensure continuing compliance on the production line. Pre-licence inspections are becoming quite common, as are complete checks of the manufacturer's quality control and, in some cases, quality-assurance systems, depending on the product in question. Once the certification organization is satisfied that the manufacturer has the ability to comply on a continuing basis, certification is granted. This normally consists of the issuing of a licence allowing the manufacturer to place a certification mark on all products that the manufacturer claims meet the particular standard on which the certification was based. The manufacturer, as part of the licensing agreement, grants the certifier the right to audit the manufacturer's production as long as the agreement is in effect. Violations of the agreement can result in cancelling of the licence, requests for recall and public disclosure; in some cases, legal action is taken by the certifier against the manufacturer. Where a manufacturer is required to have the product certified prior to sale or installation, the releasing of a sub-standard product violates not only the licence agreement but a legal statute as well. Here again, the APEO Code of Ethics has a bearing: ''a professional engineer shall make effective provision for meeting lawful standards.''

The success of such a certification program depends on the degree of acceptance of a particular certification mark by the purchaser or by the regulatory authorities. The marks of most of the agencies we have mentioned have been tried and accepted over a period of many years; in some cases the mark is recognized and accepted not only throughout Canada but internationally.

As with any system, there are benefits and drawbacks. The fact that standards take so long to develop can be restrictive; it can retard innovation, particularly in design standards rather than performance-type standards. However, for every drawback there is usually a positive benefit. A case in point was the development of standards for plastic pipe for use in the plumbing field. Prior to the 1960s plumbing inspectors across the country would not accept anything but the traditional materials, such as cast iron and copper. The industry in Canada, aware that the potential for its plastic product would be limited, turned towards the standards process to solve the problem. The standards that were developed included requirements and tests to determine the equivalency of plastic to the more traditional materials, and once products meeting the standards were available, the plumbing inspectors felt that they now had something on which to make a judgment. Thus the standard helped to advance the technology. On the other hand, again to do with plastics, the safety standard for electrical refrigerators for many years contained a requirement that the enclosure be made of metal, mainly because when the standard was originally issued no one thought that anybody would use anything but metal for the enclosure. Because the requirement was in the standard, the use of plastics was precluded and it took several years

80

for the standard to be changed and that design constraint to be removed. Under such circumstances, and where product certification is needed for legal acceptance, delay in modifying the certification standard is detrimental to both the industry and the consuming public. Fortunately, ways have been devised to expedite standard requirements for use on an interim basis pending a complete standard revision.

Looking toward the future, with our growing concerns for energy conservation and protection of the environment, the potential for more standards is virtually unlimited. With our technology becoming more complex year by year, there is every likelihood that more engineers will be required to serve on standards committees representing either users, producers, regulatory authorities or even consumers. Engineers will certainly have to work with the results of the standards system. Questions of efficiency, reliability, life expectancy, reasonable safety vs. ultimate safety, and ultimate performance will challenge these engineers and present them with unique opportunities not only to make a worthwhile contribution to the Canadian community as a whole, but also to advance the concept of professionalism and ethical behaviour.

CHAPTER 8

INTERNATIONAL ENGINEERING WORK

THE BEGINNING

When we consider engineering as "the introduction of change into the conditions of living" we realize that it has been going on since prehistoric times. Also, that there have been international, or foreign, projects since the dawn of civilization.

About eight to ten thousand years ago an agricultural revolution started in the fertile regions of Iraq and Syria and an acre of land under cultivation became able to support twenty to two hundred times as many people as before. This freed some of the people from the subsistence tasks of hunting and food-gathering and so they were able to engage in other occupations. Permanent villages grew to cities. Cities require specialists. To the tribal wizard or priest and the tribal chief were added merchants, physicians, poets, smiths; instead of building their own houses or carts or wells, people began to acquire these from specialists.

As wealth and experience developed, people undertook projects too large for a single craftsman. Organization of hundreds and thousands of workers came about. Out of this came a new class of people: the technicians and engineers who could negotiate with a king or priesthood to build a public work, a fortress, an aqueduct, a tomb; to plan the details and direct the workers.

These engineers had to be inventors as well as contractors, designers and bosses: they had to be able to imagine something new and transform the mental picture into a physical reality.

Perhaps all that does not seem to have much to do with explaining how engineers became involved historically in foreign projects. However, consider what was happening in agricultural revolution.

Agriculture required irrigation and irrigation required central administration.

Historians may argue whether empire came first and made possible large-scale irrigation or whether large-scale irrigation came first and encouraged the growth of empire. It does not matter to this discussion. What is important is that expansions of empires took place in the valleys of the Nile, Tigris, Euphrates, Indus and Hwang-ho, and technicians and engineers became involved in foreign projects. Expansion of empires meant that engineers and technicians went into "foreign service" to support both civil and military requirements.

Usually history is taught to us in terms of warrior-heroes like Achilles and Hector and the siege of Troy—but about the same time as Troy was being besieged a nameless genius invented the safety pin. Most of us know about Julius Ceasar, but who has heard of his contemporary Sergius Orato, the Roman building contractor who invented central indirect house heating? Thus the engineer in history is more often than not unnamed if not forgotten.

As civilizations grew, incentives associated with the use of engineers in foreign projects also developed. These can be categorized as military, religious, commercial, political and altruistic.

The following examples illustrate some of these aspects.

About 1000 BC, Assyrian military engineers developed the belfry, or moveable siege tower. This grew from the simple scaling ladder, which did not provide any protection to attacking soldiers as they tried to climb a fortress wall.

The fully developed Assyrian siege tower had six wheels, a lower tortoise covered with wood and hides, and a front tower with enclosed stairways and water containers to fight fires. In the tortoise a ram was suspended on chains. This siege weapon was the dominant attack device for about two thousand years, until the cannon made lofty walls useless for defence.

When Sargon II of Assyria invaded Armenia in 714 BC, he saw a form of irrigation supply not then practised in Mesopotamia. It used an underground tunnel sloping from a mountain source to bring water to the dry plains. It had the advantage of reducing losses due to evaporation. As described by James Michener in *Caravans*, ancient examples of this form of civil engineering can still be seen in Afghanistan. Today agricultural engineering is an important part of Canada's international engineering activity.

The Phoenicians living along the Lebanese coast of the Mediterranean were active engineers in shipbuilding. They developed two styles, one a long, narrow war galley, one a broad stubby merchantman, both using oars.

Engineers today have to be familiar with standards. In Greece, roads began as simple tracks with ruts worn by cartwheels. As time went on the ruts were often dug out and lined with cut stone; in Athens, each track was about 20 cm wide, 7-15 cm deep and the gauge was 137 cm. Roads were provided with sidings like railways.

In Syracuse the gauge was 150 cm. Thus a person who brought a chariot from Syracuse to Athens would find the wheels were too far apart to fit the tracks.

In 331 BC Alexander took Deinokrates, an architect from Rhodes, to Egypt and commissioned him to lay out the city of Alexandria. The Romans, during the approximately eight hundred years of the western empire, 400 BC to 400 AD, carried engineering to the far reaches of the conquered countries as well as bringing engineers to Rome. The Romans built roads for civil communications and to expedite military movements, aqueducts for water supply, merchant ships to bring cargoes from Egypt to Rome. As well, in unconquered lands like Persia, Roman engineers were in demand for civil engineering works.

Leonardo da Vinci, perhaps best known for his artistic triumphs such as the Mona Lisa, was military engineer to the Duke of Milan for eighteen years.

In the middle ages in Europe, mining and metallurgy developed with Germany taking a leading role. By 1560 AD Germany was sending mining engineers to England to mine copper near Keswick, zinc in Somerset, and to set up a brass foundry (1568) near Tintern Abbey. These imported engineers came in some cases at the invitation of English companies, sometimes to set up German companies. During the reign of Elizabeth I, German engineers came to Britain to work on hydraulic problems, including draining mines and providing water supplies to towns.

In the period 1750-1780 English engineers went to France to work in foundries, machining shops and water works.

WHY DO INTERNATIONAL PROJECTS GET STARTED?

A simple answer—international projects are started in the same manner as domestic projects. Someone needs a service or facility;

another person or organization can provide the desired service or facility.

However, in the international scene there are aspects that can have differences in degree or in type from those factors that exist for a purely domestic project.

The reasons that lead to an international project being carried out today are often the same reasons that history has shown to have existed in the past—they include military, religious, commercial, political and altruistic purposes. History tells us that most foreign projects are initiated for rational reasons; unfortunately some are started for irrational objectives or misunderstood needs.

However, lest the foregoing leave you with too pessimistic a view of human nature, let us note that not all foreign and international projects are started for selfish reasons. There have been, and are, many instances of foreign projects being initiated for purposes not simply selfish—not purely military, not just for commercial gain. In saying this we can note examples like those supported by the Marshall plan of the United States, after the Second World War, which was instrumental in the rebuilding of Europe, and Canada's Colombo Plan, which has provided financing for many countries for equipment and training.

For international projects today, the funding may come from any of a number of sources.

Consulting engineers interested in foreign work should be familiar with the operations of national and international financing agencies. Some of the principal ones are the International Bank of Reconstruction and Development (IBRD) or World Bank; International Finance Corporation (IFC), also an affiliate of IBRD; the Inter-American Development Bank (IDB); the Export-Import Bank of the United States (Eximbank); the U.S. Agency for International Development (AID); Overseas Private Investment Corporation (OPIC); the Asian Development Bank; and the African Development Bank. Except for the last two agencies, all have headquarters in Washington, D.C.

In Canada, the primary source for financing foreign projects is the Export Development Corporation (EDC), an agency of the government of Canada.

In judging whether to grant financing for a project, a lending agency generally uses the following criteria, and perhaps others also.

    (i) will the project contribute to economic development;

   (ii) is it consistent with development plans;

  (iii) is it economically and technically sound;

  (iv) are adequate self-help measures being taken;

   (v) is there ability to repay; and,

  (vi) has adequate consideration been given to financial assistance from other international or private sources?

The two main categories of projects are:

> Productive projects that will contribute immediately to economic development, such as power, transportation, ports, irrigation and agriculture.
>
>   Projects of a social or development nature; for example, water and sewerage utilities, schools, hospitals, housing.

All the lending agencies, national and international, have fairly close working relations; to a large extent all follow the above criteria and priorities, based on their collective experience and their operating policies.

   It should be noted that lending agencies such as the EDC in Canada and the Export-Import Bank of the United States have an additional objective. That goal is to facilitate the sales of goods and services by Canadian and United States firms respectively. Most countries have lending agencies with similar objectives.

   For international projects that require long-term financing, the choice, by the foreign client, as to which country will provide engineering services will often be determined by which country offers the most attractive arrangement.

ENGINEERING WORK OUTSIDE CANADA IS DIFFERENT

When considering the prospects of doing international engineering work, either as an individual or on behalf of your employer, you should investigate the rules, regulations and accepted practices at the place of that work because they could differ drastically from ours in Ontario and those in other parts of Canada. While this is just a partial checklist, here are some questions typical of what you will want answered.

   In that country:

   1) Are practising engineers required by law to hold a licence; and if so, what are the legal requirements and

qualifications the engineer must have; and how many engineers are registered in that country?

2) Will you and other foreign engineers be required, by the law of the country, to obtain a licence to practise there; and if so, what are the requirements for obtaining it; how long will it take and how much will it cost?

3) For foreign consulting engineers to practise there, are they required to have local representatives; and if so, must those representatives be engineers; must they be citizens of that country, or may they be Canadian or other non-nationals who are resident there?

4) Must there be local participation in any contract with a Canadian consulting engineer; and if so, to what extent?

5) What is the official and the commercial language in the country; what system of weights and measures is used?

6) What is the unit of currency; what is the exchange rate and how stable is it; what, if any, restrictions will be imposed on taking salary or fee out of the country?

7) What proportion of take-home pay must be paid by the employer for social costs such as social security, unemployment insurance, health and death benefits, vacation and holiday pay, year-end bonuses, retirement and severance pay?

8) What income tax rules, Canadian and host country, will apply; and what foreign-exchange restrictions will there be?

The answers to these and to the other questions, which of course there will be, will depend on the particular host country. You should do your best to find out what the answers are before making a commitment to do engineering work in a foreign country.

CHAPTER 9

COMMUNICATIONS

The art of expressing ideas by words and/or symbols.

In its broadest sense the scope of communications goes far beyond the written word and includes the many sounds of words and music, histrionics in its many forms, and eyeball to eyeball signals. However, without in any way suggesting that these other ways of communicating a message are not important, or that they are less important, the theme of this chapter is restricted to written communications.

Communications is a critical element in professional engineering practice. In any engineering undertaking, the objective and how to achieve it must be communicated, usually in words. The undertaking could be a firm or a joint venture submitting a proposal to provide the required engineering services on a major project. When such a proposal is accepted, even provisionally, there will be preliminary and feasibility studies; if it clears that hurdle there will be more studies, preparation of designs and specifications. Then will come change orders, inspection reports and eventually the final inspection and acceptance report, probably with a list of deficiencies. This is just one example that shows the importance to engineers of reports and other documents; that is, composing words to transmit thoughts—communications. Another example, while not such a major project in some respects, could be of even greater importance to a young engineer: the preparation of an application for a job.

An excellent article, "The Practical Writer," in "The Royal Bank Letter" (published by the Royal Bank of Canada, Vol. 62, No. 1 Jan./Feb. 1981), is reproduced here, with minor editorial revisions, by kind permission of the Royal Bank of Canada. That permission is gratefully acknowledged by the authors who consider the message in "The Letter" to be of particular interest and of prime importance to practising professional engineers.

THE PRACTICAL WRITER

Written words form the mainstay of communications
in organization.
But often they fail to do the job.
Here is a guide to writing that means business.
There's nothing to it but blood, sweat and tears:
then review, revise, check and double-check!

From time to time most business and professional people are called upon to act as writers. You may not think of yourself as such when you dash off a personal note or dictate a memo, but that is what you are. You are practicing a difficult and demanding craft, and must meet its inherent challenge. That is, to find the right words and to put them in the right order so that the thoughts they are intended to communicate will be understood.

The purpose of any written message is to transmit the writer's thoughts—on some subject—to the reader's mind. This is so, especially in businesses and institutions where written words carry so much of the load of communications. The written traffic in any well-ordered organization is heavy and varied—letters, memos, reports, policy statements, manuals, sales literature and other messages.

The objective is to use words in a way that serves the organization's aims. Unfortunately, often a written communication does not achieve this objective. Some writing gives rise to confusion, inefficiency, and ill-will. Almost always this is because the intended message does not get through to the receiving end because it was not presented effectively.

An irresistible comparison arises between writing and another craft that most people have to practise sometimes: cooking. In both fields there is a wide range of competence, from the great chefs and authors to the occasional practitioners who must do the job whether they like it or not. In both, care in preparation is essential. Shakespeare wrote that it is an ill cook who doesn't lick his own fingers; it is an ill writer who doesn't work at it hard enough to be reasonably satisfied with the results.

Unlike bachelor cooks, however, casual writers are rarely the sole consumers of their own offerings. Recluse philosophers and schoolgirls keeping diaries are about the only writers whose work is not intended for other eyes. If a piece of writing turns out to be an indigestible half-baked mess, those on the receiving end are usually the ones to suffer. This might be all right in a book, because the reader can toss it aside anytime. But in organizations, where written communications command attention, the recipient of a sloppy writing job must figure out what it means.

The reader is thus put in the position of doing the thinking the writer failed to do. To make others do your work for you is, of course, an uncivil act. In a recent magazine advertisement on the printed word, one of a commendable series published by International Paper Company, novelist Kurt Vonnegut touched on the social aspect of writing: "Why should you examine your writing style with the idea of improving it? Do so as a mark of respect for your readers. If you scribble your thoughts any which way, your readers will surely feel that you care nothing for them."

In the business and professional world, bad writing is not just bad manners, it is bad business practice also. The victim of an incomprehensible letter will be annoyed at best or, at worst, will decide that people who can't say what they mean aren't worth doing business with. Write a sloppy letter, and it might rebound on you when the recipient calls for clarification. Where one carefully worded letter would have gotten your message across, you may have to write two or more.

Muddled messages can cause havoc in an organization. Instructions that are misunderstood can set people off in the wrong directions or put them to work in vain. Written policies that are open to misinterpretation can throw sand in the gears of an entire operation. Ill-considered language in communications with employees can torpedo morale.

A CAREFUL WRITER MUST BE A CAREFUL THINKER

In the early 1950s the British Treasury grew so concerned with the inefficiency resulting from poor writing that it called in a noted man of letters, Sir Ernest Gowers, to work on the problem. As a result Gowers wrote an invaluable book, *The Complete Plain Words*, for the benefit of British civil servants and anyone else who must put English to practical use. (Her Majesty's Stationery Office, London, 1954.)

Gowers took as his touchstone a quotation from Robert Louis Stevenson: "The difficulty is not to write, but to write what you mean, not to affect your reader, but to affect him precisely as you wish." To affect your reader precisely as you wish obviously calls for precision in the handling of language. And to achieve precision in anything takes time.

Gowers suggested that the time spent pursuing precision more than cancels out the time wasted by imprecision. People in administrative jobs might well protest that they were not hired as writers, and that they are busy enough without having to fuss over the niceties of grammar and syntax. The answer is that an important part of their work is to put words on paper. It should be done just as thoroughly and conscientiously as anything else they are paid to do.

No one should be led to believe writing is easy. As great a genius as Dr. Samuel Johnson described composition as "an effort of slow diligence and steady perseverance to which the mind is dragged by necessity or resolution." Writing is hard work because thinking is hard work; the two are inseparable. But there is some compensation for the effort required to write well.

The intellectual discipline required to make thoughts intelligible on paper pays off in clarifying your thoughts in general. When you start writing about a subject, you will often find that your knowledge of it and your thinking about it are inadequate. The question that should be foremost in the writer's mind, "What do I want to say?" will raise the related questions, "What do I really know about this? What do I really think about it?" A careful writer must be a careful thinker—and in the long run careful thinking saves time and trouble for the writer, the reader, and anyone else concerned.

The problem is that many people believe that they have thought out ideas and expressed them competently on paper when they have not. This is because they use nebulous multi-purpose words that may mean one thing to them and something quite different to someone else. Gowers gives as an example the verb "involve," which is used variously to mean "entail," "include," "contain," "imply," "implicate," "influence," and so on. "It has . . . developed a vagueness that makes it the delight of those who dislike the effort of searching for the right word," he wrote, "It is consequently much used, generally where some more specific word would be better and sometimes where it is merely superfluous."

THE RIGHT WORD WILL ALMOST TELL YOU WHERE IT SHOULD GO

There are many lazy man's words lurking about, threatening to set the writer up beside Humpty Dumpty, who boasted: "When I use a word, it means just what I want it to mean." You should not use ambiguous words and expressions. In his book *How to be Brief*, Rudolph Flesch gives us the first commandment of practical writing: "Be Specific. Specify, be accurate, give exact details—and forget about fine writing and original style."

Style tends to take care of itself if you select the right words and put them in the most logical order; so, to a large extent, do grammar and syntax. Find the right word, and it will almost tell you where in a sentence it should go. That is not to say that grammar and syntax are not important. Words just scattered on a page would not be comprehensible. The rules of language usage also exert a degree of discipline over your thinking about a subject by forcing you to put your thoughts in logical order. Many grammatical conventions are intended to eliminate ambiguity, so that you don't start out saying one thing and end up saying something else.

Most literate people, however, have an instinctive grasp of grammar and syntax that is adequate for all ordinary purposes. The rules of usage (in English more so than in French) are flexible, changeable, and debatable; new words are invented as the language lives and grows, and a solecism in one generation becomes respectable in the next. So while grammar and syntax have their roles to play in written communications, they must not be followed so blindly that the message is not understood by the reader. Gowers quoted Lord Macaulay with approval on this score: "After all, the first law of writing, that law to which all other laws are subordinate, is this: that the words employed should be such as to convey to the reader the meaning of the writer.''

USUALLY VOCABULARY IS THE LEAST OF A WRITER'S PROBLEMS

Since words come first, an ample vocabulary is an asset in conveying meaning. Oddly enough, though, people who have difficulty getting their written message across rarely lack the vocabulary required. They know the apt words, but they don't use them. They go in for sonorous but more or less meaningless language instead. People who are perfectly able to express themselves in plain spoken language somehow get the idea that the short, simple words they use when talking are not suitable in writing. Thus where they would say, "We have closed the deal," they will write, "We have finalized the transaction." In writing, they "utilize available non-rail ground-mode transportation resources" instead of "using trucks." They get caught in "prevailing precipitant climatic conditions" instead of in "the rain." They "utilize a manual earth-removal implement" instead of "digging with a shovel." When so many words with so many meanings are being slung about, nobody can be quite sure just what the message is.

The guiding principle for the practical writer should be always use common words unless more exact words are needed for definition. Surely the reason for this is obvious. It is that if you use words that everybody knows, everybody can understand what you want to say.

A common touch with language has always distinguished great leaders. Winston Churchill comes immediately to mind; as John F. Kennedy said, he "mobilized the English language and sent it into battle." Churchill mobilized the language in more ways than in his inspiring speeches. As prime minister of Great Britain, he was that nation's chief administrator at a time when governmental efficiency was a matter of life and death for the democratic world. In August, 1940, while the Battle of Britain was at its peak, Churchill took the time to write a memo about verbiage in inter-departmental correspondence. It read:

93

> Let us have an end to such phrases as these: "It is also of importance to bear in mind the following considerations . . ." or "Consideration should be given to carrying into effect . . ." Most of these woolly phrases are mere padding, which can be left out altogether or replaced by a single word. Let us not shrink from the short expressive word even if it is conversational.

Churchill's own wartime letters and memos, reproduced in his memoirs, are models of effective English. It is interesting to speculate on how much his clarity of expression, and his insistence upon it in others, helped to win the war. He was, of course, a professional writer who had earned a living with his pen since he was in his early twenties. He was a master of the English language and, while it may seem ridiculous to exhort modern white-collar workers to write like Winston Churchill, the principles of writing he used are not hard to grasp.

Churchill was an admirer of Fowler's *A Dictionary of English Usage*, and when he caught his generals mangling the language he would direct them to it. Fowler set five criteria for good writing—that it be direct, simple, brief, vigorous and lucid. Any writer who tries to live up to these is on the right track. By keeping in mind two basic techniques you can go some way towards meeting Fowler's requirements. These are:

USE VERBS IN THE ACTIVE VOICE RATHER THAN THE PASSIVE

It will make your writing more direct and vigorous. In the active voice you would say, "The carpenter built the house;" in the passive, "The house was built by the carpenter." Though it is not always possible to do so in a sentence, use the active whenever you can.

PREFER THE CONCRETE TO THE ABSTRACT

A concrete word stands for something tangible or particular; an abstract word is "separated from matter, practice, or particular example." Churchill used concrete terms: "We have not journeyed all this way, across the centuries, across the oceans, across the mountains, across the prairies, because we are made of sugar candy." If he had couched that in the abstract, he might have said: "We have not proved ourselves capable of traversing time spans and geographical phenomena due to a deficiency in fortitude." Again, there are times when abstractions are called for by the context because there are no suitable concrete words, but do not use them unless you must.

Sticking to the concrete will tend to keep you clear of one of the great pitfalls of modern practical writing, the use of "buzz words." These are words and expressions that are used not because they mean anything in particular, but merely because they sound impressive. It is difficult to give examples of them because they have such short lives; the "buzz words" of today are the laughing stock of tomorrow. They are mostly abstract terms ending in -ion, -ance, -osity, -ive, -ize, -al, and -ate, but they sometimes take the form of concrete words that have been sapped of their original meaning. The reason for avoiding them is that their meaning is seldom clear.

Jargon presents a similar pitfall. It has its place as the in-house language of occupational groups, and that is where it should be kept. Do not use it unless you are certain that it means the same to your reader as it does to you.

Combining the active and the concrete will help to make your prose direct, simple, vigorous, and lucid. There is no special technique for making it brief; that is up to you. The first step to conciseness is to scorn the notion that length is a measure of thoroughness. It isn't. Emulate Blaise Pascal, who wrote to a friend: "I have made this letter a little longer than usual because I lack the time to make it shorter."

Use your pen or pencil as a cutting tool. No piece of writing, no matter what its purpose or length, should leave your desk until you have examined it intensely with a view to taking the fat out of it. Strike out anything that does not add directly to your reader's understanding of the subject. While doing this, try to put yourself in his or her shoes.

Be hard on yourself; writing is not called a discipline for nothing. It is tough, wearing, brain-wracking work. But when you finally get it right, you have done a service to   **95** others. And, like Shakespeare's cook, you can lick your metaphorical fingers and feel that it was all worthwhile.

You are well advised to heed the creed of the wise writer. There is no such thing as good writing, only good rewriting.

(This is the end of the Royal Bank Letter.)

STYLE IN PRACTICAL WRITING

The word style, used in connection with practical writing, is usually coupled with an adjective. So coupled, it becomes redundant or, at best, is a name for an obvious characteristic of the writing. A plain style means that the writing is plain, a concise style that it is concise, and so on. In contrast to the gross misuses in which style is taken to be the presence of gratuitous embellishment, of vogue words, or of other devices, this common simplistic usage is innocent enough, and is well understood. But it does dismiss the phenomenon of style too easily, and tends to put practical writers off their guard.

In the community of fiction writers one of the accepted doctrines is: "We do not tell readers a story; we provide the stimuli and the readers tell themselves a story."

The pleasurable effect on the reader of such stimuli is achieved by the manipulation of style by a skillful writer. But in our practical writing any such effect is adverse and part of our skill must lie in avoiding it. For in proportion to the incidence of temptation for the readers to "tell themselves the story," the writing departs from the domain of the practical.

Consider a gross example:

"Seagoing ships, upbound from the St. Lawrence or downbound from the Welland, enter Toronto harbour by the Western Gap." At best, we take this to be telling us that "deep-draft vessels use the Western Gap," and we wonder why the author has not simply said so. But it could have been even more obscure had the author put the words in a different sequence, dropped a comma, and written: "Upbound from the St. Lawrence or downbound from the Welland, seagoing ships enter Toronto harbour by the Western Gap." The writer has now beclouded the message by music—a song about ships from the four corners of the seven seas. Some train of thought, established in a preceding context, might have survived the first version, but hardly the second. The

96

first version may have been meant to be practical, but neither is in plain writing.

Now consider this example: "Keep notes in ink in a bound, stitched notebook." You will find it hard to state this rule, using any words you like, and at the same time deliberately work in an extraneous thought, without sacrificing the plainness of the instruction. If you can't do it by trying, you are not likely to do it inadvertently, and we arrive at this axiom: "Stick to plain writing, and you need not worry about your readers being diverted from the channel of thought you intend them to follow."

While not a part of the argument for plain writing, the reason this rule is used is related to ethics in engineering work. It is a good rule to follow in any situation where notes might be used later as evidence in some legal action. The precautions of keeping the notes in ink and in using a bound, stitched notebook are to prevent fudging of the notes by erasing and changing them and/or removing a page and replacing it with different notes on the page substituted.

Edmund Gosse, one of the contributors to the *Encyclopaedia Britannica*, (eleventh edition, 1910-1911), presents many and varied comments and quotations on style in literature. One is that Flaubert's "ingenious definition of style seems to strain language beyond its natural limits;" another is that "All these attempts at epigrammatic definition (of style) tend to show the sense that language ought to be, and even unconsciously is, the mental picture of the man who writes." This can be disconcerting to the unpractised practical writer. Having been assured that if you write plainly you need have no worry about the unwanted effect of style already drawn to your attention, you are now bedevilled by the suspicion that what your typist is reproducing at 80 wpm is a sort of "portrait of the artist" that may cross a hundred desks. How shall you protect yourself against this exposure, or, if you cannot, how can you render yourself more photogenic?

Plain writing offers no refuge. It is the key not to avoiding or disguising "the mental picture of the man who writes," but to the control of it. It is a control that permits the image to reveal the writer only to the extent that the writer relates to the subject written about. If others enter and are represented by the writer (boss, group, firm) what the writer says of or attributes to them must be included in the control so that they are pictured only to the extent that they relate to the matter in hand. But let us not risk "straining language;" here is an example:

97

"Pay to the Order of _____   _____ dollars"

In an age of euphemistic writing, this form has survived because the style precisely fulfils the function intended. Try adding "please," and see the style vanish before your eyes, and the image of the writer (the person who signs the cheque) slips out of focus. As it stands, let us look at what the style says.

> This conventional form was composed, not by the writer who signs it, but by the Bank. We know that, and it is visible in the style, for custom allows the bald command form (drill sergeants and the legal summons excepted) only in writing composed by the party commanded.
>
> Writers who sign the cheque say of themselves (are, in fact, forced to say of themselves when they use the form) that they have the right to command and are willing to assume responsibility for the consequences. They declare themselves, at this moment at least, one with the whole edifice of trust and probity on which such transactions are based.

No more is exposed of the writer than that which relates to the purpose of the writing, although the style transmits a lucid picture. This is the comfort offered any who may be uneasy about self-revelation in practical writing.

Gosse offers this advice: "The errors principally to be avoided in a cultivation of pure style are confusion, obscurity, incorrectness and affectation."

We have mentioned the presence of others in the picture drawn. In Robert Graves' *Claudius the God* the Roman emperor says: "There is an art in playing second fiddle. I know. I have practised it all my life." With us, this is a common position.

Often we write to express decisions that are not our own but have been taken by others. About three generations ago, in such circumstances, writers portrayed themselves by using such formal starts as "I am directed to inform you . . ." They thus declared their part in the business in the first person, and charted the course of their self-portrayal through the whole communication. Using today's less cumbersome formulation, as in writing "Our design group explains the seeming discrepancy by citing the new code requirements," the writer's position of intermediary is implied, although not stated. In both forms, the image pursued is that of a knowledgeable man or woman, able to put forward the arguments with due respect for the dignity of the party addressed and of the writer's principals.

Writing where they are themselves the authority (having presumably carried out the study or inspection that is the subject matter), young engineers must get away from the pupil-teacher style they used, and probably were encouraged to use, in the undergraduate laboratories. It is no longer acceptable to display knowledge just to prove that you have it. For sophisticated readers, elements of classroom recitation reflect only immaturity. Writing on your own authority demands that you construct, for any situation, an answer to the age-old question, "Who am I?"

To the imaginative writer it has been said, "If you would have me weep, you must weep first." For us, if we would add to our practical writing an image of the writer that will illuminate it, as it were, for the reader, we must establish the image in our own minds first, before we select and adopt the norms of expression that will render and sustain it.

The "norms of expression" a writer uses are selected from a memory store, reviewed by a critical faculty, modified, rejected or accepted—all at high speed, all within the brain. Range and variety of the items in store are gained by our reading, and the critical faculty is nurtured by the discernment we apply to the reading. But, considered as a source for augmenting the store or for sharpening our perception, our reading may be random and repetitive. The program, then, consists of a regime—fortunately an easy and entertaining one—of reading books that illustrate "norms of expression," for the most part by discussing hundreds of key words and often setting them in various contexts, showing not so much what is right and wrong, but suggesting what the example is saying to an observant eye and ear about the subject matter and, frequently, about the writer. Three of these are listed below. All are famous, all are written with the gentleness and humour that scholarship seems to achieve in teaching. The listing is in alphabetical order of the authors' surnames, so no favourite is indicated; we recommend all three as an inexpensive little array of bedside companions. Read them and enjoy them!

Fowler, *Modern English Usage* (Oxford).
Gowers, *The Complete Plain Words* (Pelican).
Strunk and White, *The Elements of Style* (Brett-MacMillan).

CHAPTER 10

QUESTIONS

This chapter consists of thirty-six questions typical of those used on the examination paper in professional practice and ethics at the APEO annual examinations during the past several years. Notes appropriate to the examination are:

APEO Code of Ethics to be supplied.
No textbooks or other aids permitted.
If you have any doubt as to the meaning of any question, give a clear statement of how you have interpreted it.

The nature of the subject is such that is not enough to give a simple yes or no answer to the question, "Was it unethical?" for the engineer to do whatever it was the question states that he or she did. The candidate is expected to appreciate the ethical considerations involved and to explain how the yes or no answer was arrived at. Also, because of the complexity of a given situation, it may not be an open-and-shut case. Often the answer should be such as, "Yes, but we should also consider this way of looking at it," with some discussion from that point of view. The mark the examiner assigns will depend not only on the analysis and reasoning presented by the candidate but on how the answer is reported.

Wherever appropriate in the context, the singular is intended to include the plural and the masculine to include the feminine.

1. A technical paper based on extensive research was selected by an engineering society as the best in its field. Awards were made to two of the three co-authors of the paper at a national meeting of the engineering society, but the senior author was not given an award

because of a rule of the society that restricts its awards to those who are members at the time a paper is submitted. The non-member co-author was not given credit at the award presentation.

(a) Was it unethical for the society not to give an award to one of the co-authors?

(b) Did the society officers and award recipients have any obligation to give credit to the non-member co-author?

2. An owner retained engineer Smith for certain engineering services under written agreement but before Smith had completed the work the owner notified him that the agreement was being terminated. Subsequently the owner retained engineer Jones to do the same work. Smith informed Jones, in writing, that termination of his agreement had been by unilateral action of the owner and that he, engineer Smith, had not accepted it. Was it unethical for Jones to undertake the work in view of the unilateral termination of Smith's agreement, without his consent and in spite of his objections?

3. John Doe, an engineer employed by a testing laboratory, represents his firm on a standards committee for automobile products. All but two of the ten members of this committee are engineers. After much deliberation the committee arrived at a consensus but Mr. Doe was violently opposed to the end result and registered his objection. After careful consideration of this objection the committee passed the standard for formal publication. Subsequently the laboratory received a contract to test automotive products to the standard and Mr. Doe was assigned the job of supervising the tests and compiling the final report which indicates that the samples meet the requirements of the standard, and signing the report on behalf of his firm. He objects because he considers that his signature on a report attesting to the conformance of a product with a standard indicates that he endorses the standard. In this case he does not consider the standard to be proper.

Is he correct in his assumptions? What action should he take?

4. An engineer was retained by a government department

to make a study of computer-programming methods and techniques for the economical extraction of certain metals from ore. He undertook extensive investigations, conducted experiments and submitted a comprehensive report, which contained detailed recommendations to solve the problems set out in his assignment. He was paid an appropriate fee for his services and the project was terminated. The government published the report and made it available to the public. Two years later the engineer was approached by a commercial mining company that had a problem similar in scope and content to that which he had studied under his contract with the government. He was requested by the mining company to act as its consultant and to recommend methods to improve its operation in this type of work.

Does he have an ethical obligation to inform the mining company, before he accepts the assignment, of the existence and availability of the report he had prepared for the government?

5. For many years the XL Company has manufactured a product that enjoys a high rating in the industry and with the public. Competing manufacturers have now introduced a similar product of lower quality at lower cost, and this competition has caused a serious decline in the sales of the product manufactured by XL Co. To meet this competition XL Co. instructs its engineers to redesign its product so that it may be made available to the market at a lower price. Upon receiving these instructions some of the engineers question whether such an action would be consistent with the Code of Ethics, because a lower-quality product under the same brand name would mislead the public into accepting a product of lesser quality in the mistaken belief that it meets the high quality standards with which the product has been associated in the public mind for many years.

Do the engineers have a proper interest and ethical obligation to protest the company's decision, or to refuse to redesign the product?

6. An engineer enters into a contract with a public body whereby he agrees to conduct such field investigations

and studies as may be necessary for a determination of the most economical and proper method for the design and construction of a water-supply system, to prepare an engineering report, including an estimate of the cost of the project, and to estimate the amount of bond issue required.

The contract provides that, if the bond issue passes, the engineer will be paid to prepare plans and specifications and supervise the construction, and will be paid a fee for his preliminary services. If said bond issue should fail, the public body would not be obligated to pay for the preliminary work. The public body is prohibited by law from committing funds for the preliminary work until the bond issue is approved.

May an engineer ethically accept a contingent contract under these conditions?

7. Engineers of Company A prepared plans and specifications for machinery to be used in a manufacturing process and Company A turned them over to Company B for production. The engineers of Company B, in reviewing the plans and specifications, came to the conclusion that they included certain miscalculations and technical deficiencies of a nature that the final product might be unsuitable for the purposes of the ultimate users, and that the equipment, if built according to the original plans and specifications, might endanger the lives of persons close to it. The engineers of Company B called the matter to the attention of appropriate officials of their employer who, in turn, advised Company A of the concern expressed by the engineers of Company B. Company A replied that its engineers felt that the design and specifications for the equipment were adequate and safe and that Company B should proceed to build the equipment as designed and specified. The officials of Company B instructed its engineers to proceed with the work.

Under these circumstances what should the engineers of Company B do now?

8. An engineer working with a gratuitous service organization with the objective of "assisting those working to raise living standards in developing areas of the world" has inquired as to the extent to which he may ethically

103

provide engineering assistance through this volunteer organization. A number of inquiries for technical assistance are from overseas field workers associated with various volunteer organizations who are seeking technical advice related to problems in the areas of the world in which they are stationed.

A typical request for assistance directed to the engineer was for a method of improving a primitive African water supply, which consisted of uncovered holes intercepting ground water. Those requesting such technical advice are not in a position to pay for it.

Is it ethical for an engineer to provide technical advice to persons or organizations through a volunteer organization?

9. An owner retained an architect to prepare plans and specifications for a building, using the standard CCA/RAIC contract form. The architect, in turn, retained a structural engineer for the structural portion of the plans and specifications. The building was erected. Both professionals completed their respective portions of the contract, except the execution of the required certificate of compliance. During the progress of the work, the owner made progress payments to the architect, and the architect paid the appropriate amount from his payments to the structural engineer. However, when the building was completed and ready for occupancy, the owner still owed and refused to pay the architect a substantial sum that was due under the contract, and the architect accordingly owed the structural engineer a proportionate amount. The owner alleged that there had been several deficiencies in the work of the architect and refused to pay him the balance due. The owner requested the city officials to issue to him an occupancy permit, and they requested the architect, who in turn requested the structural engineer, to certify that the structural system was completed in compliance with the applicable building code and regulations. Such a certification is required before the city may issue an occupancy permit to the owner. The structural engineer refused to provide the certification until he had been paid for his services.

Is it unethical for the engineer to refuse to provide the certification that would enable the owner to secure the occupancy permit, on the ground that he has not been paid for his services?

10. An engineering firm with extensive experience in the design of industrial equipment and processes proposes to establish a value-engineering division, under which it would offer to clients a value-engineering service. The plan of operation contemplates offering to clients in the industrial field a review of their designs, equipment, products, processes, and so on. Following such review, the firm would suggest to the client revisions in the design or production procedures that would produce the same result at less cost to the client without sacrifice of quality or safety. If such savings are realized, the client would pay the firm a portion of the savings, determined by negotiation before the service is rendered, in accordance with the extent of work involved. If the client determines that the proposed changes are not feasible or desirable for any reason and does not utilize the suggested changes it is not obligated to pay the firm for these services.

    Is this proposed method of operation ethical?

11. Engineer A is employed by an industrial corporation. His immediate supervisor, Engineer B, is chairman of a civic committee responsible for retaining an architect to design a civic facility. When Engineer B received the completed plans and specifications from the architect, he directed Engineer A to review them in order to (1) gain knowledge, (2) suggest improvements, (3) assure their compliance with the specified requirements.

    (a) Does the instruction of Engineer B to Engineer A violate the Code of Ethics?

    (b) Will it be unethical for Engineer A to carry out the instructions given him by Engineer B?

12. An injured worker is involved in a proceeding before a workmen's compensation board relative to the amount of compensation to which he is entitled. The determination rests in large measure upon the conclusion of the board as to certain technical details related to the accident. The worker asks an engineer to appear before the board as an expert witness, but states that he is indigent and cannot afford to pay the engineer for his services.

    The engineer is willing to assist the worker, but asks

whether he may ethically do so: (a) on a contingent-fee arrangement, whereby he would be paid a percentage of the amount received by the worker, or (b) as a compassionate and gratuitous action.

Is it ethical for an engineer to provide services as an expert witness for an indigent client on either a contingent or free basis?

13. A company that regularly undertakes projects for the federal government employs several registered professional engineers. During slack periods this company "stockpiles" its engineering staff to the extent necessary so as to have them available when needed for future work and assigns them to clerical and other subprofessional duties. During these assignments the direct supervisors of the engineer involved are not engineers.

    Is it a violation of the Code of Ethics for the engineers to serve in clerical and sub-professional capacities during slack periods of their employer's operations?

14. A manufacturing company has contracted to develop and produce a completely automated mass-transportation system. Public safety would be endangered by a failure of the system, if one were to occur. A series of engineering tests were carried out on the various components during the development period, but one major assembly did not perform satisfactorily. The engineer who is manager of the department responsible for the project reported the failure to his superiors. He was told, however, that in order to meet the contract commitments the equipment would be shipped to the client without informing the client of this failure. The engineer objected to this decision and learned subsequently that shipment to the client had been made.

    What, if any, further action should the engineer take under these circumstances?

15. An employee, X, worked for Engineer A for five years, during which time X progressed from draftsman to designer. A expects that, with further training and experience, X will continue to progress. Engineer B, in the same city, approached X directly and offered him a

job with B's firm without notice to, or discussion with, A. X accepted the offer and, after giving two weeks' notice to his employer, A, left to work with B.

Did B act unethically?

16. An engineer is employed by a large consulting engineering firm and his work includes the designing and specifying of electrical equipment. He owns shares in a large, well-known and reputable electrical manufacturing company; his share holding amounts to less than one-tenth of one percent of the company's outstanding shares.

    Is it a violation of the Code of Ethics when, in the course of his work, this engineer selects and specifies equipment made by the company in which he holds stock?

17. A member of the city council is chairman of the council's finance committee, which deals with and makes recommendations regarding appropriations for projects undertaken by the city. One such project is a pollution-abatement project, for which funds were allocated. The chairman of the council's finance committee is one of the principals in a consulting-engineering firm that has established a good reputation in the pollution-control field, and the firm submitted a proposal to the council to provide the engineering services required for the project under consideration.

    Under these circumstances, was it ethical for this consulting-engineering firm to offer to undertake this engineering work?

18. An engineer employed by Company A is assigned by his supervisor to develop processing equipment for the manufacture of certain chemical products. In his previous employment with Company B, the engineer had participated in the development of similar equipment. The technical information concerning the equipment has not been published in the technical press, or otherwise released. By virtue of his previous involvement in its development the engineer is familiar with the equipment and the principles of its design. His superiors in Company A suggest that this knowledge will be useful in developing similar equipment for their use and

107

expect him to make his knowledge concerning the particular equipment available to Company A to aid in the development of the similar equipment.

May the engineer ethically apply his knowledge to the development of equipment for his present employer based on experience and information gained in similar work for a previous employer, without the consent of the previous employer?

19. Engineer X is one of the partners in a consulting engineering firm, XYZ, whose services include designing, specifying and supervising the installation of mechanical-electrical systems in buildings and factories. X proposes to form a company that would contract to provide system operation and maintenance services for such facilities. He would be the major shareholder in this company and expects that most of the contracts the company would get would be for work on installations that had been engineered by XYZ.

    Would the operation of the proposed company, in the manner envisaged, be consistent with the requirements of the Code of Ethics? Comment on the various points involved.

20. Engineer A learned that an engineering position with the CBC was vacant and he applied for the job. After the interview he was told by the interviewer that he was being considered favourably for the appointment, but he was not hired nor was any commitment made to him. Engineer B learned of the opening and, while knowing that A was being considered favourably for the appointment, applied for the same position. In presenting his own qualifications, B made no reference whatever to A. When A learned that B had applied for the position, while knowing that he was being considered favourably for it, he complained to the Practice and Ethics committee of APEO, alleging that this action by B was unethical.

    Was B's action unethical?

21. Most of the duties of an employee at a consulting engineering firm are related to finding and exploring prospects for engineering service contracts for the firm. This employee is not a professional engineer; he is paid

a salary plus a commission on the contracts he arranges for the firm.

(a) Is it ethical for an engineering firm to have a non-engineer as a representative to discuss engineering aspects of a project and contract negotiations with a client?

(b) Is it unethical for a firm to employ a non-engineer as a representative to solicit contracts for its services?

(c) Is it unethical to compensate such a representative on a commission basis?

22. An engineer becomes aware that one of the products his company produces does not meet the standards required by law, and when he brings this to the attention of his immediate superior, he is either overruled or ignored.

What action should the engineer take?

Does it make any difference if the safety of the public is not involved?

23. A building contractor engaged a professional engineer to design and prepare drawings for the formwork and scaffolding for a reinforced-concrete building, to meet the requirements of construction-safety legislation. The engineer did this, and affixed his seal and signature to the original tracings, which he turned over to the contractor. Was this acceptable professional practice?

Later the contractor engaged the engineer to inspect the scaffolding as built. He found that in many significant parts his design had been ignored, and the contractor's superintendent had built it the way he thought it should be built.

What should the engineer do? Discuss this situation and the engineer's professional responsibility for the safety of the workers.

24. A company has a large, integrated operation that includes consulting engineering services, construction, and manufacturing. Its brochure and advertisements state that it is engaged in all of these activities and that it will provide all or any portion of these services, as may be the wish of a client. The company usually acts for clients on major projects such as dams, power

plants or factories, and has a separate division for each of the main functions. All of its engineering operations are directed by registered professional engineers.

Because of its other activities, is the practice of consulting engineering by this company a violation of the Code of Ethics?

25. A member of APEO is working in a foreign country for a client building a power station. He is acting as technical advisor to the client. The client is directly supervising all construction labour.

    The client does not have any apparent safety procedures for his labour; no hard hats, no safety shoes, in some cases no shoes. Holes in floors do not have safety barricades. The conditions are clearly such that they would be unacceptable in Canada. Even assuming the poor safety conditions will not affect the technical aspects of the power station, clearly they affect the safety of workers.

    Would it be ethical for the Canadian engineer not to take any action? What kind of action could he take? Do you consider that it is likely that the poor safety practices could affect only the safety of workers and not have any relation to the technical aspects of the power station?

26. The engineering staff of a municipality prepared designs and specifications for the paving of a six-mile stretch of road. Two designs were prepared, one for concrete pavement and the other for asphalt, with the understanding that the two would be of equal quality and would give equal service. Tenders for the concrete pavement averaged about fifteen percent higher than those for asphalt. All tenders were rejected and the engineers were instructed by the chief engineer to revise the concrete design to a lower standard, but not to change the asphalt design. In the second set of tenders the bids on the revised design for concrete pavement were about seven per cent higher than the new asphalt bids. The chief engineer recommended that the contract be let to the low bidder on the revised concrete design.

    (a) Was it ethical for the chief engineer to recommend the award of a contract based on a design to a lower standard, at a higher price?

(b) Was it ethical for the chief engineer to have the design revised to a lower standard in order to reduce the price of one material but not the other?

27. A large multinational corporation selected and interviewed three consulting engineering firms in Ontario regarding the engineering services it would require in connection with the designing of, and the supervision of the construction of, a new plant the corporation was planning to have built in Ontario.

Each firm, in its proposal, stated that the fee would be that recommended by APEO for complete engineering services on a project such as the one described.

Later, the corporation asked each firm to state the amount by which it would reduce its fee if the corporation provided the following portions of the overall engineering services:

(a) preliminary engineering studies and a report that contains a suggested layout for the plant;

(b) all field engineers and inspectors required to supervise the construction of the plant.

The three firms got together and discussed this request and agreed on the amount (the same figure for each of the three) by which they would reduce the overall fee to allow for the data and field staff to be provided by the corporation.

Was it unethical for these three firms to confer and agree on an amount to allow for these data and field staff?

Would it have been competitive bidding for each of the firms to determine independently an amount by which it would reduce the fee?

28. A young member of APEO who graduated in chemical engineering is employed by the Ontario branch of a large multinational chemical company. The Ontario branch manufactures, among other things, a wide variety of solvents, paints and other types of finishes, using formulas developed in the research laboratory located at the American head office of the company. An Ontario manufacturing company is a principal customer. A Ministry of Labour inspector has required the company to provide the ministry with information about all the ingredients used in the products turned out by the plant, particularly regarding their possible risk to

the health of the factory workers. The professional engineer knows that a key ingredient in one of their products has been linked to a large number of cancer cases among the employees of an American customer. He has been ordered to prepare a report to meet the requirements of the Ministry of Labour inspector.

What course of action should he take?

29. Basically, the Code of Ethics sets the standard of conduct for the professional engineer, yet often the employers of engineers are not familiar with the Code of Ethics or even aware of its existence.
    (a) Why then is the Code important to industry?
    (b) What could be the consequences to a company of using persons who are not registered professional engineers in engineering positions?
    (c) Is the Code of Ethics compatible with the goals of industry?

30. An engineer in private practice was retained by a client to design and to supervise the construction of a warehouse. Some time later he was asked by another client to provide professional engineering services for a warehouse almost the same as that previously designed by him, except for those minor changes that were required to conform the building with the site. This client suggested that the fee be lower than that charged for the original design services because the engineer could use his same design with only minor changes. The APEO recommendations do not cover this point.

    For this re-use of his design, would it be ethical for the engineer to charge a fee substantially less than that recommended by APEO?

31. An engineer who is an expert in his field of technology is often called upon to serve as technical advisor on behalf of parties in lawsuits. His assignment is to provide the attorney for the party that retained him with expert analysis and advice on the technical reasons for the failure that led to the damage. He may also be called upon to testify as an expert witness in support of his findings on the technical aspects of the case.

    The usual arrangement is that he is paid for these services on a per-diem basis. For this case he has been requested to provide similar services for a plaintiff on the basis of being paid a percentage of the amount recovered by the plaintiff. If the judgement is in favour of the defendant he will not be paid for his services. The attorney for the plaintiff is handling the case on a similar arrangement for his fee.

Would it be ethical for an engineer to act as a technical adviser, to serve as an expert witness in a lawsuit on a contingent-fee basis?

32. After having been employed by consulting engineer B for several years, engineer A terminated his work with B and started his own practice of consulting engineering. Later B learned that some of his sub-professional employees were doing work for A on their own time. B is of the opinion that the outside work by his sub-professional employees is so extensive that it adversely affects their productivity while they are working for him.

Did A act unethically by employing the sub-professional employees of B under the conditions stated?

33. A strike by its production and maintenance workers seriously disrupted the operations of an oil company, including the operation of one of its refineries. During the disruption, officers of the company assigned some of the company's engineers to duties normally carried out by the workers who were on strike in order to continue the operation of the refinery on a reduced basis.

Was it a violation of the Code of Ethics for these engineers to perform these duties?

34. For several years an extensive and costly flood-control and hydroelectric project in Canada has been considered by a provincial government. There is no generally accepted opinion as to which of two different design approaches should be adopted. One of these would use one high dam while the other would use a series of low dams.

A meeting was held by a committee of the provincial legislature to hear and consider comments and recommendations regarding these two proposed design approaches.

A professional engineer representing the provincial power commission reported that studies he and his professional colleagues had made indicate that from an engineering standpoint the more efficient solution is the one with a series of low dams.

Another professional engineer representing a private power company reported that his engineering analysis indicates a more effective and less expensive solution is obtained using one high dam.

Each presented voluminous engineering data to support his conclusion and openly disagreed with the analysis and recommendations of the other.

Discuss this situation and whether there was a violation of the Code of Ethics by one or the other engineer by criticizing the work and the statements of the other engineer in a public meeting.

35. A municipality in Ontario owns an arena and was ordered by a provincial government inspector to have the structural adequacy of its arena roof inspected and evaluated by a member of APEO. It engaged engineer A and his report stated that the roof trusses were not strong enough to support safely the snow and wind loading stipulated for that location by the then current Ontario Building Code. Engineer A was then asked to prepare a design to strengthen the roof trusses and to estimate the cost, which he did.

The municipality learned from an adjacent municipality that engineer B, whom it had engaged to investigate a similar building, had proposed a much simpler and cheaper method of repair and so it decided to consult engineer B, and engaged him.

Comment on the ethics of the behaviour of engineers A and B and on the responsibilities of the two municipalities to provide for the safety of the people who will use the arenas.

36. Why are there both a legislative Act and a Code of Ethics to govern the members of the engineering profession in Ontario? How do the items covered by the Act differ from those covered by the Code? Comment on how the Act and the Code overlap, and how they differ.

CHAPTER 11

SOME ADVICE TO EXAMINATION CANDIDATES AND ANSWERS TO SOME QUESTIONS

We recognize that, when writing an examination, your prime objective is to obtain a "pass" standing. The advice we offer here includes that objective and goes beyond it.

The essence of this message is: do your best!

You should study the introductory remarks in Chapter 10.

At the start of the examination, what you should do first is read and make sure you understand the notes at the beginning of the examination paper. Then you should read through all of the paper to find out what, if any, options you have. You will find that to have been a wise investment of your time.

Probably there will be some selection. Choose the questions you feel you would do better on, and in what sequence to answer them. You will find that time spent on this process at this stage will be time well spent. Based on your knowledge of your speed at writing examinations you should know whether the time available is likely to be a significant factor. If there is some probability that you will not have ample time for composing and writing your answers to the questions selected, you should establish a target schedule and hold to that schedule within reasonable tolerances. Do not get carried away by your special interest in one of the questions and spend so much time on it that you will have to skimp on the others.

Because of the ambiguity of so many words and expressions in the English language the intent of a statement or question is too often misinterpreted by the reader or listener. Not long ago in Canada, an air-traffic controller ordered a snowplow operator to "clear the runway." He intended his instruction to be "get your equipment and yourself out of the way and off the runway

because there is an airplane coming in to land.'' Instead the operator interpreted the message to mean ''clear the snow off the runway.'' The plane hit the plow and forty-three people were
killed.

As stated in the introduction to Chapter 10, if you have any
doubt as to the meaning of any question, you should give a clear
statement of how you have interpreted the question.

Answer the question asked. That may seem to be a redundant
suggestion but all too often a candidate has an interest in a point
that is only slightly relevant to the situation described in the question and goes off on a tangent. To illustrate this point refer to
question 34. It may be interesting to you to speculate on what
technical analyses and conclusions may have been advanced by
either or both engineers, and which of the two proposals would
be selected by a competent engineer after a thorough, unbiased
engineering and financial study of the proposed project. These
are interesting matters to contemplate but neither is what the candidate is asked to do in the final paragraph of question 34.

As you are aware, APEO has developed and published a Code
of Ethics, which sets out some of the many obligations of the
members of the profession. This Code is reproduced in this book
and, as stated in the preamble to Chapter 10, will be supplied
with the examination paper in Professional Practice. Because a
copy of the Code will accompany the examination paper there is
no need for candidates to memorize it. You should, however,
have studied it and should be aware of all its implications.
Because the Code is available to the examiner also, it would not
be worthwhile, nor would it be rewarding, to lengthen your
answer to a question by quoting at length from it. You could refer
to an item in the Code by number and subscript.

To become a worthy member of the engineering profession
you must possess many talents. Of the many requirements, two
of the more important characteristics are competence and honesty. Together they constitute the foundation on which the profession is based.

In this chapter the authors present what they consider to be
acceptable answers to a selected sampling of the questions in
Chapter 10. The numbers refer to the numbers of the questions in
that chapter. The reader is referred to the introductory comments
in Chapter 10. For the examination the APEO Code of Ethics will
be supplied but no other books or aids will be permitted.

Most of the questions on the examination paper will be related to a situation that will require your analysis of, and deliberation regarding, the ethical aspects of one or more of the professional-engineering practice features of that situation. The case-studies approach is usually an effective way to carry out such an exercise. Here is an example:

A CASE STUDY

A member of APEO is working in a foreign country for a client who is building a power station. The client supervises directly all of the construction labour. The member of APEO is technical adviser to the client.

The client does not have any apparent safety procedures for his labour: no hard hats, no safety shoes, in some case no shoes. Holes in floors do not have safety barricades. The conditions are clearly such that they would be unacceptable in Canada.

Question 1. While assuming the poor safety conditions will have no effect on the technical aspects of the power station, clearly they can affect the safety of the workers. Is it ethical for the Canadian engineer not to take any action? What kind of action can he take?

Question 2. Do you consider that it is likely that the poor safety practices would affect only the safety of the workers and not have any effect on the technical aspects of the power station?

This "case study" differs in minor detail only from Question 25 in Chapter 10 of this book and is typical of the world outside of the classroom. It separates students and practising engineers into two distinct groups. One group consists of those who think there are absolute answers and seek to find them, often by methods that are little better than guessing. Those in the other group take a systematic approach to assess the information presented in the case. It is important to use a systematic method; achieving an answer is almost incidental. By using systematic procedures you will always develop a reasonable answer.

Notice that the result is described as reasonable—there may be more than one answer. This possibility of having more than one answer seems to surprise many students. It should not be a surprise—life's like that. Just as there may be more than one way to go to work, more than one strategy to achieve an objective, more

117

than one way to pay for a purchase, often there can be several solutions to a problem.

The following notes outline one method of looking at a case systematically. There are five parts to the method:

> identify the problem; identify the question; list the facts; list postulates; inter-relate the pertinent facts and useful postulates.

IDENTIFY THE PROBLEM

The first two parts to this method might appear to mean the same thing but the "problem" and the "question" refer to quite different aspects of the case. One way to view these two aspects, the problem and the question, is to think of them as: a) the problem is what you are given; b) the question requires you to give something back—a reasonable answer.

Another way to think of these aspects is that if there was not a problem, there would not be any questions; the problem leads to the questions.

In looking back at the case, the first paragraph describes an engineer working on a foreign project that involves a power station. This paragraph provides some information but does not indicate the existence of a problem.

The second paragraph describes some safety-related matters. Indeed there are serious construction-safety deficiencies reported. This clearly seems to be a problem. Hence the first step of the method seems to be satisfied by identifying a problem of construction safety.

Can there be more than one problem in a case? The answer is yes. However, having found at least one problem it is not forbidden to move on to the second step of the method.

IDENTIFY THE QUESTIONS

In this case two questions appear to be clearly identified and labelled as question 1 and question 2.

Cases can be presented without highlighting the question so clearly, nor do questions have to be at the end of the case, as in this example.

Moreover: is it true that there are only two questions? Under question 1 there are really two questions and these are fairly obvious, as they are in separate sentences, both ending in question marks. Thus in total there seem to be three questions in this case.

LIST THE FACTS

The facts are things or information given in the case that can be considered to be true. In this case the list includes:

It is a foreign project.
There is a client.
The client supervises the labour force.
The engineer is a technical adviser to the client.
The engineer is a Canadian and a member of APEO.
The project is a power station.
There are no apparent safety procedures: no hard hats; no safety boots; no safety barricades.
These working conditions would be unacceptable in Canada.
The Canadian engineer knows the conditions are unsafe.

Having listed all the facts that seem to be given in the case the next step is to list postulates.

LIST POSTULATES

Listing postulates requires some use of imagination. In fact, in the first instance it sometimes can be a useful exercise to put down all the possibilities that come to mind, no matter how fanciful or unlikely they may be. It is always possible to cut down a long list by eliminating unreasonable or inappropriate items afterwards.

What are the postulates? Postulates are hypotheses—any things, conditions, features, attributes, knowledge, actions or other features that might be possible and that you can imagine might be true in the context of the case but that were not given in the case.

In this instance the following postulates are included, and, of course, there may be more.

There are safety procedures but the engineer has not seen them.

119

Safety treatment of labour is not important in this country.

The client does not understand safety practices.

There are safety laws but the client is ignoring them—the laws are not enforced.

There are safety laws and these are usually enforced—there is some other reason the client is not following safety practices on this job.

Poor safety practices will not affect the technical aspects.

Poor safety practices will affect the technical aspects.

The first question is a matter of professional ethics as implied by the wording of the question.

Conversely, the first question has nothing to do with professional ethics but may be pertinent to social ethics.

Canadian ethics, professional or social, do not apply in the foreign country.

The Canadian engineer can offer safety-training instruction or guidance.

The Canadian can seek advice from or can notify safety agencies in the foreign country.

There are engineers on the project from countries other than Canada.

It is not a matter of ethics but of commercial interest.

Even if it is not a matter of ethics, this would not be a reason to not take some action.

In the first question, ethics is not really an important consideration if at all a valid part of the question.

The Canadian engineer has no authority to take any action.

The Canadian can exercise persuasion in some form to influence the client.

The Canadian is himself endangered by the poor safety practices.

The list of postulates can be a long one. The important result, however, is that some of the postulates will almost always begin to lead to possible answers to the question.

INTER-RELATING FACTS, POSTULATES AND QUESTIONS

This last step can be considered as a time to discuss facts and postulates that appear to relate properly to the problem. One way to start this is by eliminating ideas that do not seem to be pertinent. For example, it probably does not matter to the problem of safety that the project is a power station. It could have been a chemical plant or an oil refinery with the same kind of problem.

Another way is to consider facts and postulates that tie together. The postulate that not only the local workers but the Canadian also may be endangered by poor safety practices indicates there is a strong incentive for the Canadian to take some action even though it is not a matter of ethics. The argument that poor labour-safety practices will affect the technical aspects might help convince the client that safety is important. Volunteering to provide a training program in safety practices is a specific action that can be taken. Other possible actions include seeking help from local government agencies and co-operating with engineers from other countries working on the site to encourage safety practices. Setting a proper example is a form of persuasion.

The above discussion is not the only line of reasoning that may be applied in this case study. A second theme could be developed: since the Canadian is a consultant, among the duties for which he has been retained is to institute safety procedures and training. Further, it can be postulated that the client is receptive, but the failure has been one by the Canadian engineer to fulfill his contractual obligation; if so, professional ethics is a consideration.

SUMMARY

This suggested approach is one way to analyze a case but is not the only way. What is important is to be systematic.

By some of the arguments advanced in this analysis, it is reasonable to conclude that, in the situation reported, there is no convincing evidence of any violation of the Code of Ethics even though the working conditions are definitely undesirable and unacceptable by Canadian standards. But when the situation is considered from another point of view, ethics is indeed a significant factor. It may not make much difference which argument prevails; in either case the same action would be appropriate and could be taken. That action would include persuasion, co-operation and training.

Safety of the local workers and of the Canadian engineer himself and the expectation that the completed project would be of a higher quality, and consequently a better reputation-builder, would be the incentive to stimulate the action.

121

ANSWERS TO SOME QUESTIONS

As stated previously, wherever appropriate in the context the singular is intended to include the plural and the masculine to include the feminine.

Because of the nature of the subject and the broad scope of the considerations relevant to the situation presented, the answer given is not always the only acceptable answer to that question.

1. (a) No, the society has its own rules and is not bound by a code of ethics of some other association.

    However, it would have been appropriate and surely it would have been the polite thing to do to give some credit to the senior author, even though he was not eligible for an award because he was not a member of that particular engineering society at that time.

   (b) The same comments apply to the society officers as to the society in a) above. Perhaps an argument can be advanced that there was no obligation because of the rule of the society, but certainly it would have been logical and courteous to give some credit to the senior author for his part in the research. This reasoning considers that the "senior" author was not just "older" than the other two but that he did have a major role in the project on which the research paper was based.

    Continuing the assumption that he had been an active member of the research team, certainly the two award recipients did have an obligation to give credit to their colleague. See Code 1(a) and 1(c).

2. Before being able to determine whether B acted unethically by undertaking to do the work, it is necessary to know whether A's connection with the work had been terminated. Because the statements by the owner and by engineer A about termination of agreement were contradictory, B had an obligation to find out which statement was true before he undertook the work. What were the facts?

    Loyalty to a confrere might sway B's judgement towards believing engineer A's story, while wishful thinking might make the owner's version more attractive and so easy for B to believe, especially if he wanted the work badly enough. However, neither loyalty nor wishful thinking is a sound substitute for critical examination. Under circumstances such as those cited, it may be necessary to retain proper legal counsel to interpret the agreement in question. If there has been valid termination of the agreement between the owner and A, it was ethical for B to undertake the work; if the termination was not valid then it was unethical for B to do what he did. See Code 1(a), 1(c) and 5(f).

3. There are two points to be considered in this question and we should deal with them separately.

   One point is whether the standard is proper; the other is whether the products meet the requirements of that standard.

   John Doe's assumption that his signature on a report that stated that the samples conformed with the requirements of the standard would indicate that he endorsed the standard is incorrect. It would indicate that the samples conformed with the requirements of the standard, and that only.

   What he should do is get on with the job, conduct the tests and report on them.

   Further, if he feels strongly enough that the standard should be reviewed, and perhaps revised, he should take the appropriate steps that are provided for that to be done.

4. To determine the answer to this question we must consider what different factors are involved and the various possibilities.

   When the engineer-consultant was working with the government there was a requirement for confidentiality of information between consultant and client. This is no longer a factor since the report has been published and is available to the public.

   One might take the position that not being aware that the report is available is evidence that the company is in need of, and should retain, a consultant to bring it up to date on such matters. If this be so, why bother with such details as a two-year-old report? There was a requirement for confidentiality of information between

123

consultant and client until the project was terminated. This is no longer a factor since the report has been published and is available to the public.

Another possible situation is that, during the time between when the study was made for the government and now, there may have been substantial advances in that specialty. One must realize that "the company" per se is difficult to deal with; any deal must be made with some person who is acting for the company. It is not improbable that the officer of the company who had communicated with this engineer was a top-flight metallurgical engineer who was familiar with the study the consultant had made for the government. The impression created would be not too favourable if the consultant appeared in any way to be withholding information by not mentioning the earlier report.

Even without the careful consideration of these various relevant factors, the answer seemed obvious at the start. Yes, he should inform the company of the availability of the report before he accepts the assignment; honesty and integrity must predominate. See Code 1(a), 1(c) and 4(a).

5. The question states that the competing similar product is of lower quality at lower cost, and that the engineers at XL Co. were instructed to redesign their product so that it may be made available to the market at a lower price.

Much depends on how we interpret the words "made available at a lower price." We may speculate that the redesigning of the XL Co. product would introduce a safety hazard but there is nothing in the wording of the question to suggest that that would be so.

It may be that the original design was unduly elaborate and perhaps the most significant effect of redesigning the product would be to simplify the manufacturing process and result in a product that not only would cost less to produce (and consequently could be made available at a lower price) but one that was a better product.

Because there is no convincing evidence that there is any sound reason the instructions "to redesign the product" should not be carried out, we conclude that the engineers *do not* have "a proper interest and ethical obligation to protest the company's decision" nor to refuse to follow the instructions they were given to redesign the product so that it could be made available at a lower price.

9. This question describes a situation where the architect has contracted with the owner to provide certain services. Also, the structural engineer has contracted with the architect to provide certain of those services. While not stated explicitly in the question, the usual arrangement is that there is no contractual relationship between the owner and the engineer and I have assumed that to be so in this case.

   The matters to be considered in this situation are more than the ethics; they include strategy in interprofessional relations, tactics in negotiating, marketing of consulting engineering services and the law of contract.

   One significant question is: "In the contract between the architect and the structural engineer, is the signing of the certificate of compliance listed as one of the services to be provided?"

   If so, it would be unethical for the engineer not to provide the certificate because his work would not have been completed until he did.

   If, however, signing that certificate had not been listed but had been considered to be an incidental detail, it would *not* be unethical for him to refuse to execute the certificate because he had not been paid for his services. [Code 5(f).] Whether that refusal would be good business tactics is another matter, which he should consider. In this respect one must realize that any delay in the collection of fees is a much more important factor in 1982 than it was in 1918 because interest rates now are more than three times what they were then.

10. We must consider different features of the proposal; some have ethical considerations while others are more a matter of business practice. Because the expression "value engineering" may mean different things to different people, to answer this question we must analyze the proposal carefully.

The proposal is that engineering services will be provided on a "contingent-fee" basis. That is: if the client is not satisfied with and does not adopt the recommended revisions in design and/or procedures, no fee will be charged.

One could argue that this contravenes 5.(f) of the code of ethics, which states that a professional engineer shall uphold the principle of adequate compensation for engineering work. The rebuttal to that argument is that the prospect of the "portion of the saving" to be paid to the engineer by the client is "adequate compensation," and, further, that the engineer is prepared to bank on the worth of the "revisions in the design or production procedures" that would be suggested by his report.

Another comment might be made: that while the proposed arrangement may not be unethical, it is not sound business practice. That point of view could be disputed. This somewhat unusual approach might be the start of a successful and continuing client-engineer relationship.

In conclusion, the proposal is *not* unethical.

11. The status and authority of engineer B with his employer, the industrial corporation, is not stated explicitly in the question and I have interpreted the situation to be that the officers of the corporation are aware of and approve of him being chairman of that civic committee and spending time on such an activity. It is quite probable that such participation in civic affairs is of benefit to the public image of the corporation.

    Under these conditions:

    (a) The instructions given by engineer B to engineer A would not violate the Code of Ethics. Code 1(a), (b) and (c), 2(e) and (f).

    (b) It would *not* be unethical for engineer A to carry out these instructions. He should, however, take whatever steps are necessary to ensure that the architect is informed, either by engineer B or by the secretary of the civic committee, that his plans and specifications are to be reviewed for the purposes stated. A prudent engineer A would require that this information be transmitted in writing and that he receive a copy of the written communication, which he should keep in his files. Also, he should take whatever action may be necessary to be informed, by the proper authority or officer within the corporation, that it will be in order for him to spend his time (time paid for by the corporation) on this assignment. Code 1(a) and (c).

14. The question states that public safety would be endangered by a failure of the system, if one were to occur. Because of this situation, it would be a violation of the Code of Ethics for an engineer who had any responsibility in the project not to take every reasonable precaution to guard against a "failure of the system"—items 1(a), (b), (c) and 2(e).

   Because the assembly failed to pass the final tests, the engineer had an obligation to report this to his superior, and it is stated in the question that he did that.

   When told that the equipment had been shipped without the purchaser being informed of the unsatisfactory test result, the engineer is faced with an ethical problem.

   There is some probability that the assembly test was not appropriate and that the system was indeed suitable and safe, but it is more probable that such a speculation is just wishful thinking and that the poor performance of the assembly in the test was because of some deficiency in the assembly.

   Shipment having already been made, the engineer demands of his management that the purchaser be informed, at least, that satisfactory shop-test results have been obtained only for the components, and that the purchaser's acceptance test of the system must be made before public safety can be considered covered. The purchaser must be informed that the shop test of the assembly was unsatisfactory, saying in what respect.

   The engineer is bound to insist that his company do no less than this; the company is going to be liable for any additions or alterations to the system anyway, if these have to be made to meet the contract specifications. To thus make a virtue of necessity is good business for the company, and the action is vital to the reputation of the engineer.

   If the company refuses to so warn the purchaser, the

127

engineer will have to tell his employer that he is ethically bound to report the matter. At this stage he should report to his superior in writing, with a further statement that, if proper action is not taken by his employer, he will report the situation to an occupational health and safety inspector of the Ontario ministry of labour, responsible for the safety of such systems. The employer's refusal is unlikely. If the employer persists in refusal, the engineer will have to do what he says he will do. If his employment is terminated, he could probably bring action for wrongful dismissal.

18. The main considerations in the context of the situation reported are the meanings of the words "development," "ethics" and "knowledge."

    Included in the definition of an engineer we find "one who contrives, designs," and so the development of the processing equipment is engineering work.

    Items 3(a) and 3(b) of the Code of Ethics may be applicable as the engineer progresses with the design of the equipment.

    Any knowledge acquired by a person is his and he may make use of that knowledge if he wishes to, provided that by so doing he does not contravene some code, custom, law or regulation.

    It is usual for an engineer to be employed because of experience he has had. It is hoped and expected that the knowledge and training he obtained through that experience and training will have made him more capable, and hence more valuable to his employer.

    Because this is a usual practice we conclude that it is "accepted practice" and that, yes, the engineer may ethically apply *his* knowledge to the development of equipment for his present employer.

    Items 3(a) and 3(b) of the code of ethics include some points that the engineer should bring to the attention of Company A, his present employer.

    The question states that "the technical information concerning the equipment has not been published in the technical press, or otherwise released," but we do not know whether Company B has patented or otherwise imposed any effective legal restrictions on the use of any of the features of the processing equipment.

We must realize that while the engineer may ethically apply *his knowledge* to the development of equipment for his present employer, he has an obligation to bring to the attention of his present employer the possibility of the existence of such restrictions and what could be the consequences of violating them if they do exist.

21. The situation reported is not unusual in consulting practices. The three parts to the questions are whether each of three different features of the situation is ethical or unethical. Whether a feature is usual or unusual may be of interest to us but has little, if any, relevance to the questions asked.

    (a) We shall defer answering this part until after parts b) and c) have been answered, because the answers to them provide useful input in considering this one.

    (b) In the profession/business of consulting engineering, many different services are performed and several of them do not require engineers. Among these are: some scientific studies; public-relations activities; financial controls; legal matters; secretarial duties; staff recruitment. It is logical to consider the locating and arranging assignments for the firm to be another such service that someone who is not a professional engineer could do quite properly. That is not to say that the person might not be a professional engineer, but that he need not be. Considering the facts stated, it is evident that this is the business arrangement between the firm and the representative and no evidence has been presented to suggest that both parties are not in agreement with that arrangement.

    The code of ethics, item 5(f), requires that "A P.Eng. shall uphold the principle of adequate compensation for engineering work." It should be noted, however, that this employee is not a professional engineer and so is not subject to the rules of the Code, and further that there is no evidence that he does not consider the compensation to be adequate. After all, he agreed to the business deal; otherwise he wouldn't be working at the job.

And so the answer to this part of the question is: No, it is not unethical to employ a non-engineer in this role, but it should be noted that the non-engineer should not be misrepresented as being an engineer.

(c) Item 5(d) stipulates that "A P.Eng. shall not attempt to gain an advantage . . . by paying or accepting a commission." Because "he is paid a salary plus an achievement bonus," the arrangement would then be viewed in an entirely different light.

This is a fine example of the ambiguity of certain words in the English language. It is much more reasonable to consider the compensation package to be "a salary plus an achievement bonus." And so: No, it is not unethical to compensate such a representative on an achievement-bonus basis (sometimes called a commission).

(a) Considering the analyses and answers in b) and c), it follows that the answer to a) is: Yes, it is ethical for an engineering firm to have a non-engineer as a representative to discuss engineering aspects of a project and contract negotiations with a client, provided that he is not misrepresented as being an engineer.

23. No, it was not acceptable professional practice. There was a real danger that changes would be made to what was shown on the tracings and that some of these changes would result in some features of the framework and scaffolding not being as required by the safety legislation. Because the engineer no longer had control of the drawings, the contractor could have made changes for main material and connection details and the engineer could be held responsible for these changes because his seal was on them. The engineer might have been able, by some cumbersome procedures, to establish that the changes had been made without his authority or permission and consequently that he should not be held responsible for them, but perhaps he could not escape the responsibility. Certainly it was not sound practice.

After he had inspected the scaffolding and had learned that in many significant parts his design had been ignored, he should investigate those parts that did not conform with his design. Just because a detail differed from his design would not be sufficient reason to reject it but the engineer would have to be satisfied that, even if different, that way of doing it met the safety requirements so as to ensure the safety of the workers. The engineer should inform his client, the contractor, in writing, that the placing of the concrete should not be started before all these changes in the formwork and scaffolding, which he had listed in his review, had been completed, reinspected and accepted by him.

24. It is stated in the question that the three main functions of the company are consulting-engineering services, construction, and manufacturing; and that all of the engineering operations are directed by registered professional engineers. Undoubtedly, such an arrangement could be abused and there would be opportunities for unprofessional action and collusion because of the common ownership. That is not to say, however, that there would be such behaviour.

   In fact, such opportunities for misbehaviour exist regardless of the ownership of an organization carrying on any one of those three functions. The practice of consulting engineering, as such, by this company is not a violation of the Code, but there is always the possibility that an engineer employed by this or any other company might violate the Code.

   It should be noted that a company does not have any obligation under the Code of Ethics. The Code imposes obligations on a member of the APEO and he, in turn, may have some influence on the actions of his employer—the company.

26. (a) It was not ethical for the chief engineer to recommend the award of the contract that he did. See Code, 1 and 6(b). There must have been some bias in judgement or some undisclosed non-technical reason for the chief engineer to feel that the concrete design must be used rather than asphalt, notwithstanding "the understanding the two would be of equal quality and would give equal service." The instruction "to revise the concrete design to a

131

lower standard but not to change the asphalt design,'' could reasonably be interpreted as evidence of a conflict of interest or of incompetence.

(b) It was not ethical for the chief engineer to give the instructions he did to the engineers, to revise the concrete design only. See Code, 3(c) and 6(b).

28. Of particular significance in this question is the statement that the engineer *knows* that a key ingredient in one of the products *has been linked to a large number of cancer cases*.

We must consider how he became aware of that knowledge and whether the source of the information is dependable. While this is not what is asked, an obvious related question is: Why did not this young engineer do something about the situation before the company was asked by the inspector from the ministry of labour to provide the information stipulated? Even without the particular statements in items 1(a), 1(b), 1(c) and 2(a) of the Code of Ethics, we realize that a person in a position of trust, such as this young engineer is, should be mindful of public-health requirements.

The proper and necessary action for this engineer to take is to prepare his report stating the ''facts'' as he understands them to be and submit the report to the person who ordered him to prepare it. The report should provide the information requested and should include a statement that one of the ingredients in one of the products has been linked to a large number of cancer cases. Perhaps the linkage was mere speculation by some undependable publicity-seeking investigator, but perhaps it was a conclusion after a thorough and meticulous study by a competent investigator; the wording of the question does not clarify this point.

The engineer should anticipate a situation where that person objects to the reference to the ''fact'' or ''suspicion'' that the ingredient in question has been linked to a large number of cancer cases and may wish to have that omitted from the report. If that situation arises, the engineer must insist that this reference be retained in his report. If this is not done he must report the information directly to the appropriate officer in the ministry of labour, even though such action by him may mean that he will be dismissed by his employer.

29. (a) Engineering work and those who do that work make up a large part of today's industrial activity. Because of the importance of this, anything that will enhance the quality of that work and the dependability of those who do it is of definite value to the industry. The APEO expects its members to respect the rules of the Code of Ethics and administers the Act in such a way as to achieve this. As a result, most members of the association do behave in accordance with the spirit of the Code; this has brought about a situation where the Code is considered to be a "standard" for ethical behaviour by professional engineers. For this reason, aside from industry's dependence on the professional engineer, it owes much to his Code of Ethics for what it has done to enhance the dependability of the P.Eng. who is such an important factor in the industrial process.

(b) There are two aspects to be considered in response to this question.

One of them has legal implications: If, indeed, the meaning of "engineering positions" is that the law at the place of work requires that these positions be held by registered professional engineers, the situation is illegal and subject to the applicable statutory penalties.

The other is concern with the ability of the persons to do the work. The technology of the work to be done may be such that for the work to be done properly anyone doing it must have the qualifications that are required for admission to an association of professional engineers. Technical or technological incompetence could have a serious, adverse effect on the company's operations, because without this competence there would be a greater probability of a lack of appreciation of such things as the significance of obsolescence in a manufacturing process. This is just one of many examples of the adverse effects of the lack of adequate engineering input.

(c) The brief answer to this is yes, in the case of reputable industrial firms, which means, fortunately, most firms in Canada, and the reasons are as presented more fully in response to a). There are, of

133

course, unusual situations where those conditions and relationships do not exist. At times a fly-by-night industry will have shady—perhaps even illegal—objectives that are in conflict with those of the Code of Ethics.

31. Refer to Code item 4(a). If the engineer were to disclose to a court of law that the fee for his services (read "evidence") was to be contingent upon the decision of the court, it would quite definitely classify his evidence and his opinion as prejudiced. For this reason, the answer to the question is simply no, it would not be ethical for an engineer to serve as an expert witness in a lawsuit under the conditions described in the question, especially if he tried to keep secret his fee arrangement.

32. "Moonlighting" is the word used to describe the situation presented in this question. As in so many of the cases where there is moonlighting, it would be unusual if A and B were to agree that, yes, it was unethical, or, no, it was not unethical, for A to employ B's sub-professional employees under these circumstances.

    The APEO manual of professional practice deals with moonlighting by professional-engineer employees but not by non-professionals. In the situation referred to in this question, we are told that B is of the opinion that the moonlighting by his employees causes them to be less productive while working for him than they would be if they were not doing that after-hours work. Whether that lower productivity is real or just fancied by B would be difficult, if not impossible, to determine.

    The question states that B *learned* that some of his employees were doing this work with A, so we may conclude that A did not tell him.

    In view of this assessment of the situation, yes, it was unethical of A to employ B's sub-professional staff under the circumstances stated.

APPENDIX

THE SONS OF MARTHA

The Sons of Mary seldom bother, for they have inherited
    that good part;
But the Sons of Martha favour their Mother of the careful
    soul and the troubled heart.
And because she lost her temper once, and because she
    was rude to the Lord her Guest,
Her Sons must wait upon Mary's Sons, world without end,
    reprieve, or rest.

It is their care in all the ages to take the buffet and cushion
    the shock,
It is their care that the gear engages; it is their care that the
    switches lock.
It is their care that the wheels run truly; it is their care to
    embark and entrain,
Tally, transport, and deliver duly the Sons of Mary by land
    and main.

They say to mountains, "Be ye removed." They say to
    the lesser floods, "Be dry."
Under their rods are the rocks reproved—they are not
    afraid of that which is high.
Then do the hill-tops shake to the summit—then is the bed
    of the deep laid bare,
That the Sons of Mary may overcome it, pleasantly
    sleeping and unaware.

They finger death at their gloves' end where they piece
    and repiece the living wires.
He rears against the gates they tend: they feed him hungry
    behind their fires.
Early at dawn, ere men see clear, they stumble into his
    terrible stall,
And hale him forth like a haltered steer, and goad and turn
    him till evenfall.

To these from birth is Belief forbidden, from these till
  death is Relief afar.
They are concerned with matters hidden—under the
  earthline their altars are—
The secret fountains to follow up, waters withdrawn to
  restore to the mouth,
And gather the floods as in a cup, and pour them again at a
  city's drouth.

They do not preach that their God will rouse them a little
  before the nuts work loose.
They do not teach that His Pity allows them to drop their
  job when they dam'-well choose.
As in the thronged and the lighted ways, so in the dark and
  the desert they stand,
Wary and watchful all their days that their brethren's days
  may be long in the land.

Raise ye the stone or cleave the wood to make a path more
  fair or flat—
Lo, it is black already with blood some Son of Martha
  spilled for that!
Not as a ladder from earth to Heaven, not as a witness to
  any creed,
But simple service simply given to his own kind in their
  common need.

And the Sons of Mary smile and are blessed—they know
  the Angels are on their side.
They know in them is the Grace confessed, and for them
  are the Mercies multiplied.
They sit at the Feet—they hear the Word—they see how
  truly the Promise runs.
They have cast their burden upon the Lord, and—the Lord
  He lays it on Martha's Sons!

Rudyard Kipling chose his poem "The Sons of Martha," written
in 1907, to describe dramatically the great responsibilities of
engineers.

CODES/CANONS OF ETHICS

There is much more to the ethical aspects of professional engineering practice than the rules listed in a code of ethics.

Just as it would be absurd to believe that you were a mathematician because you could recite the multiplication table, or even if you were competent to punch the proper keys on a computer in the proper sequence to get the answer to a particular problem; so also it would be absurd to believe that you had a thorough and proper comprehension of the ethical aspects of professional engineering practice because you had memorized and could recite a code of ethics.

Not only must a professional engineer know what the Code requires but he must be aware of, and comprehend, the significance of its various stipulations.

This Appendix contains the code or canons of ethics of each of the eleven professional engineering associations and the Ordre in all of the provinces and territories in Canada, listed alphabetically from Alberta to the Yukon.

In each case permission to publish the material has been granted by the association or the Ordre.

ASSOCIATION OF PROFESSIONAL ENGINEERS, GEOLOGISTS AND GEOPHYSICISTS OF ALBERTA

CODE OF ETHICS

1 A professional engineer, geologist or geophysicist shall recognize that professional ethics are founded upon integrity, competence and devotion to service and to the advancement of human welfare. This concept shall guide his conduct at all times.

DUTIES OF THE PROFESSIONAL ENGINEER, GEOLOGIST, OR GEOPHYSICIST TO THE PUBLIC

A professional engineer, geologist or geophysicist shall
2 have proper regard in all his work for the safety, health and welfare of the public;
3 endeavour to extend public understanding of engineering, geology and geophysics and their places in society;
4 where his professional knowledge may benefit the public, seek opportunities to serve in public affairs;
5 not be associated with enterprises contrary to the public interest or sponsored by persons of questionable integrity;
6 undertake only such work as he is competent to perform by virtue of his training and experience;
7 sign and seal only such plans, documents or work as he himself has prepared or carried out or as have been prepared or carried out under his direct professional supervision;
8 shall express opinions on engineering, geological or geophysical matters only on the basis of adequate knowledge and honest conviction.

DUTIES OF THE PROFESSIONAL ENGINEER, GEOLOGIST OR GEOPHYSICIST TO HIS CLIENT OR EMPLOYER

A professional engineer, geologist or geophysicist shall
9 act for his client or employer as a faithful agent or trustee;

139

10 not accept remuneration for services rendered other than from his client or his employer;

11 not disclose confidential information without the consent of his client or employer;

12 not undertake any assignment which may create a conflict of interest with his client or employer without the full knowledge of the client or employer;

13 present clearly to his clients or employers the consequences to be expected if his professional judgment is overruled by other authorities in matters pertaining to work for which he is professionally responsible.

DUTIES OF THE PROFESSIONAL ENGINEER, GEOLOGIST OR GEOPHYSICIST TO THE PROFESSION

A professional engineer, geologist or geophysicist shall

14 endeavour at all times to improve the competence, dignity and prestige of his profession;

15 conduct himself towards other professional engineers, geologists and geophysicists with fairness and good faith;

16 not advertise his professional services in self-laudatory language or in any other manner derogatory to the dignity of his profession;

17 not attempt to supplant another engineer, geologist or geophysicist in an engagement after definite steps have been taken toward the other's employment;

18 not use advantages of a salaried position to compete unfairly with another engineer, geologist or geophysicist;

19 not exert undue influence or offer, solicit or accept compensation for the purpose of affecting negotiations for an engagement;

20 build his professional reputation on the basis of the merit of services offered and shall not compete unfairly with others or compete primarily on the basis of fee, without due consideration for other factors;

21 advise the Council of any practice by another member of his profession which he believes to be contrary to this Code of Ethics.

Latest Revision Date Shown 1978

ASSOCIATION OF PROFESSIONAL ENGINEERS OF BRITISH COLUMBIA

CODE OF ETHICS

14 Preamble—The following is prescribed as the Code of Ethics of the Association, and the Engineer is bound by its provisions just as he is bound by the provisions of the Engineers Act, 1979 and by the Bylaws of the Association.

The professional engineer shall act at all times with fairness, loyalty and courtesy to his associates, employers, employees and clients, and with fidelity to the public needs. He shall approach his work with devotion to high ideals, personal honour and integrity.

The purpose of the Code is two-fold:

(1) To give general statements of the principles of honourable conduct which, over the years, members of the profession of engineering have come to accept as required of each member in order that he may fulfill his duty to the public, to the profession, and to his fellow members.

(2) To give some specifics in the sub-sections, both of required standards and prohibited actions, in order that they may act as a guide, to the intent of the general statements. These specifics, it is emphasized, are only some examples of the broad principles upon which members of this profession must appraise and govern their own conduct.

The following Code of Ethics is promulgated as a general guide and not as a denial of the existence of other duties equally imperative, but not specifically included.

SECTION 1

The Engineer will be guided in all his professional relations by the highest standards of integrity.

(a) He will be realistic and honest in the preparation of all estimates, reports, statements and testimony.

(b) He will not distort or alter facts in an attempt to justify his decisions or avoid his responsibilities.

(c) He will advise his client or employer when he believes a project will not be successful or in the best interests of his client or his employer or the public.

141

(d) He will not engage in any work outside his salaried work to an extent prejudicial to his salaried position.

(e) In the interpretation of contract documents, he will maintain an attitude of scrupulous impartiality as between parties and will, as far as he can, ensure that each party to the contract will discharge the duties and enjoy the rights set down in the contract agreement.

(f) He will not use his professional position to secure special concessions or benefits which are detrimental to the public, his clients or his employer.

SECTION 2

The engineer will have proper regard for the safety, health and welfare of the public in the performance of his professional duties. He will regard his duty to the public safety and health as paramount.

(a) He will guard against conditions that are dangerous or threatening to life, limb or property on work for which he is responsible, or if he is not responsible will properly call such conditions to the attention of those who are responsible.

(b) He will present clearly the consequences to be expected if his engineering judgment is overruled.

(c) He will seek opportunities to work for the advancement of the safety, health and welfare of his community.

(d) He will guard against conditions which are dangerous or threatening to the environment and he will seek to ensure that all standards required by law for environmental control are met.

SECTION 3

The Engineer may promote and advertise his work or abilities provided that:

(a) The advertising preserves the public interest by reporting accurate and factual information which neither exaggerates nor misleads.

(b) The advertising does not impair the dignity of the profession.

(c) Statements do not convey criticism of other engineers directly or indirectly.

SECTION 4

The Engineer will endeavor to extend public knowledge and appreciation of engineering and its achievements and will endeavor to protect the engineering profession from misrepresentation and misunderstanding.

(a) He will not issue statements, criticisms, or arguments on engineering matters connected with public policy which are inspired or paid for by private interests, unless he indicates on whose behalf he is making the statement.

SECTION 5

The Engineer may express an opinion on an engineering subject only when founded on adequate knowledge and honest conviction.

(a) In reference to an engineering project in a group discussion or public forum, he will strive for the use of pertinent facts, but if it becomes apparent to the engineer that such facts are being distorted or ignored, he should publicly disassociate himself from the group or forum.

SECTION 6

The Engineer will undertake engineering assignments for which he will be responsible only when qualified by training or experience: and he will engage, or advise engaging, experts and specialists whenever the client's or employer's interests are best served by such service.

(a) He will not sign or seal plans, specifications, reports or parts thereof unless actually prepared by him or prepared under his supervision.

SECTION 7

The Engineer will not disclose confidential information concerning the business affairs or technical processes of any present or former client or employer without his consent.

SECTION 8

The Engineer will endeavor to avoid a conflict of interest with his employer or client, but when such conflict is unavoidable, the Engineer will fully disclose the circumstances to his employer or client.

(a) He will inform his client or employer of any business connections, interests, or circumstances which may be deemed as influencing his judgment or the quality of his services to his client or employer.

(b) He, while a member of any public body, will not act as a vendor of goods or services to that body.

SECTION 9

The Engineer will uphold the principle of appropriate and adequate compensation for those engaged in engineering work.

(a) He will not normally undertake or agree to perform any engineering service on a free basis, except for civic, charitable, religious, or nonprofit organizations when the professional services are advisory in nature.

(b) He will not compete improperly by reducing his usual charges to underbid a fellow engineer after having been informed of that engineer's charge.

SECTION 10

The Engineer will not accept compensation, financial or otherwise, from more than one interested party for the same service, or for services pertaining to the same work, unless there is full disclosure to and consent of all interested parties.

(a) He will not accept financial or other considerations, including free engineering designs, from material or equipment suppliers as a reward for specifying their product.

(b) He will not accept commissions or allowances, directly or indirectly, from contractors or other parties dealing with his clients or employer in connection with work for which he is responsible.

SECTION 11

The Engineer will not compete unfairly with another engineer by attempting to obtain employment or advancement or professional engagements by taking advantage of a salaried position, or by criticizing other engineers or by other improper or questionable methods.

(a) He will not attempt to supplant another engineer in a particular employment after becoming aware that definite steps have been taken toward the other's employment.

(b) He will not offer pay, or agree to pay either directly or indirectly, any commission, political contribution, gift, or other consideration in order to secure work.

(c) He will not solicit or accept an engineering engagement on a contingent fee basis if payment depends on a finding of economic feasibility or other preconceived conclusion.

SECTION 12

The Engineer will not attempt to injure maliciously or falsely, directly or indirectly, the professional reputation, prospects or practice of another person.

(a) He will not accept any engagement to review the work of a fellow engineer except with the knowledge of and after communication with such fellow engineer, where such communication is possible.

(b) He will refrain from expressing publicly an opinion on an engineering subject unless he is informed as to the facts relating thereto.

(c) Unless he is convinced that his responsibility to the community requires him to do so, he will not express professional opinions which reflect on the ability or integrity of another person or organization.

(d) He will exercise due restraint in his comments on another engineer's work.

(e) If he considers that an engineer is guilty of unethical, illegal or unfair practice, he will present the information to the Registrar of the Association.

(f) An engineer is entitled to make engineering comparisons of the products offered by various suppliers.

SECTION 13

The Engineer will not associate with or allow the use of his name by an enterprise of questionable character, or by one which is known to engage in unethical practice.

(a) He will not use association with a non-engineer, a corporation, or partnership as a "cloak" for unethical acts, but must accept personal responsibility for his professional acts.

SECTION 14

The Engineer will give credit for engineering work to those to whom credit is due, and will recognize the proprietary interests of others.

(a) Whenever possible, he will name the person or persons who may be individually responsible for designs, inventions, writings, or other accomplishments.

(b) When an engineer uses designs supplied to him by a client or by a consultant, the designs remain the property of the client or consultant and should not be duplicated by the engineer for others without express permission.

(c) Before undertaking work for others in connection with which he may make improvements, plans, designs, inventions, or other records which may justify copyrights or patents, the engineer should enter into a positve agreement regarding the ownership of such copyrights and patents.

SECTION 15

The Engineer will co-operate in extending the effectiveness of the profession by interchanging information and experience with other engineers and students, and will endeavor to provide opportunity for the professional development and advancement of engineers in his employ or under his supervision.

(a) He will encourage his engineering employees in their efforts to improve their education.

(b) He will encourage engineering employees to attend and present papers at professional and technical society meetings.

(c) He will urge his qualified engineering employees to become registered.

(d) He will assign a professional engineer duties of a nature to utilize his full training and experience, insofar as possible.

(e) He will endeavor to provide a prospective engineering employee with complete information on working conditions and his proposed status of employment, and after employment will keep him informed of any changes in them.

SECTION 16

The Engineer will observe the rules of professional conduct which apply in the country in which he may practise. If there be no such rules, then he will observe those set out by this code.

INTERPRETATION

15 In the event of any dispute as to the meaning or intent of these Bylaws, the interpretation of the Council shall be final, subject to the right of Appeal as contained in Section 32 of the Act.

Where the word "Act" appears in the foregoing Bylaws, it shall include the Engineers Act and all subsequent Amending Acts, unless the context otherwise requires.

REPEAL OF OLD BYLAWS

16 Upon the coming into force of the foregoing Bylaws, all the Bylaws of the Association previously in force shall stand revoked.

Latest Revision Date Shown 1979.

ASSOCIATION OF PROFESSIONAL ENGINEERS OF THE PROVINCE OF MANITOBA

PROFESSIONAL ENGINEERS CODE OF ETHICS

1. PREAMBLE

1.1 Honesty, justice and courtesy form a moral philosophy which, associated with mutual interest among men, constitute the foundation of ethics. The professional engineer should recognize such a standard, not in passive observance, but as a set of dynamic principles guiding his conduct and way of life. It is his duty to practise his profession according to this code of ethics.

1.2 As the keystone of professional conduct is integrity, the professional engineer will discharge his duties with fidelity to the public, his employers, and clients, and with fairness and impartiality to all. It is his duty to interest himself in public welfare, and to be ready to apply his special knowledge for the benefit of mankind. He should uphold the honour and dignity of his profession and also avoid association with any enterprise of questionable character. In his dealings with fellow engineers he should be fair and tolerant.

2. DUTY TO THE STATE

2.1 The professional engineer owes a duty to the state, to maintain its integrity and its law.

2.2 He shall at all times act with candour and fairness when engaged as an expert witness and give, to the best of his knowledge and ability, an honest opinion based on adequate study of the matter in hand.

3. DUTY TO THE PUBLIC

3.1 The professional engineer shall regard the physical and economic well-being of the public as his first responsibility in all aspects of his work.

3.2 He shall advise on, design or supervise, only such projects as his training, ability and experience render him professionally competent to undertake.

3.3 He shall guard against conditions that are dangerous or threatening to health, life, limb or property on work for which he is responsible, or if he is not responsible, shall promptly call such conditions to the attention of those who are responsible.

3.4 He shall not associate himself with, or allow the use of his name by, an enterprise of doubtful character.

3.5 He shall not issue one-sided statements, criticism, or arguments on engineering matters which are initiated or paid for by parties with special interests, unless he indicates on whose behalf he is making the statement.

3.6 He shall refrain from expressing publicly an opinion on an engineering subject unless he is aware of all the related facts.

3.7 He shall not permit the publication of his reports, or parts of them in a manner calculated to mislead.

3.8 He shall on all occasions seal plans and specifications which legally require sealing and for which he is professionally responsible and ethically and legally entitled to seal, whether he acts in the capacity of a consultant or as an employee.

3.9 He shall sign or seal only those specifications and plans for which he is professionally responsible and which have been prepared by him or under his personal direction.

---

4.   DUTY TO HIS CLIENT OR EMPLOYER

4.1 The professional engineer shall employ every resource of skill and knowledge that he commands to perform and satisfy the engineering needs of his client or employer in a truly worthy manner.

4.2 He shall act in professional matters for each client or employer as a faithful agent or trustee.

4.3 He shall ensure that the extent of his responsibility is fully understood by each client or employer before accepting a commission.

4.4 He shall not disclose any information concerning the business affairs or technical processes of clients or employers without their consent.

4.5 He shall engage, or advise each client or employer to   149 engage, and shall co-operate with, other experts and specialists whenever the client's or employer's interests are best served by such service.

4.6　He shall present clearly the consequences to be expected from deviations proposed, if his engineering judgment is overruled by other authority, in cases where he is responsible for the technical adequacy of engineering work.

4.7　He shall inform his clients of any business connections, interest or circumstances which may be deemed as influencing his judgment or the quality of his services to his clients, before accepting a commission.

4.8　He shall not allow an interest in any business to adversely affect his decision regarding engineering work for which he is employed, or which he may be called upon to perform.

4.9　He shall not receive, directly or indirectly, any royalty, gratuity, or commission on any patented or protected article or process used in work upon which he is retained by his client, unless and until receipt of such royalty, gratuity or commission has been authorized in writing by his client.

4.10　He shall not accept compensation, financial or otherwise, from more than one interested party for the same service, or for services pertaining to the same work, without the consent of all interested parties.

4.11　He shall not be financially interested in the bids as or of a contractor on work for which he is employed as an engineer unless he has the written consent of his clients or employers.

4.12　He shall not accept commission, allowances, or fees, directly or indirectly, from contractors or other parties dealing with his client or employer in connection with work for which he is responsible, except proper engineering fees paid to him by the contractor for engineering work done prior to the award of the contract for a project for which the client subsequently appoints him consulting engineer, and then only if the client has been fully informed of the transaction prior to his appointment.

5.　DUTY TO THE PROFESSION

5.1　The professional engineer shall think highly of his profession and its members, its history and traditions and shall act in a manner worthy of its honour and dignity at all times.

5.2 He shall constantly strive to broaden his knowledge and experience by keeping abreast of new techniques and developments in his field of endeavour and to maintain his reputation for skill and integrity.

5.3 He shall participate in extending the effectiveness of the engineering profession by interchanging information and experience with other engineers and students, and by contributing to the work of the engineering societies, schools and scientific and engineering press.

5.4 He shall not advertise in an unprofessional manner by making misleading statements regarding his qualifications or experience.

5.5 He shall endeavour to extend public knowledge of engineering, shall discourage the spreading of unfair or exaggerated statements regarding engineering, and shall strive to protect the engineering profession collectively and individually from misrepresentation and misunderstanding.

5.6 He shall present appropriate information to the registrar of the association, if he considers that a professional colleague is engaging in unethical, illegal or unfair practice.

6. DUTY TO HIS COLLEAGUES

6.1 The professional engineer shall take care that credit for engineering work is given to those to whom credit is properly due.

6.2 He shall uphold the principle of appropriate compensation for those engaged in engineering work, including those in subordinate capacities, as being in the public interest by maintaining the standards of the profession.

6.3 He shall endeavour to provide opportunity for the development and advancement of engineers and technical people in his employ.

6.4 He shall not attempt to injure falsely or maliciously, directly or indirectly, the professional reputation, prospects or business of another engineer.

6.5 He shall not accept any commission to review the work of a fellow engineer except with the knowledge of, and after communication with, such fellow engineer, where such communication is possible.

6.6 He shall refrain from criticizing another engineer's work in public, recognizing the fact that the engineering societies and the engineering press provide the proper forum for technical discussions and criticisms.

6.7 He shall not attempt to supplant another engineer after definite steps have been taken towards the other's employment.

6.8 He shall not compete with another engineer by reducing his usual fees or salary after having been informed of the other's fees or salary.

6.9 He shall not accept employment by a client, knowing that a claim for compensation or damages, or both, of a fellow engineer previously employed by the same client and whose employment has been terminated, remains unsatisfied, or until such claim has been referred to arbitration, or issue has been joined at law, or unless the engineer previously employed has neglected to press his claim legally, or the council of the association gives its assent.

6.10 He shall not use the advantages of a salaried position to compete unfairly with another engineer.

6.11 He shall always uphold the principle of a proper and separate fee being charged for engineering services for which he is responsible, whether acting as an independent consultant or as an employee of a firm supplying services in addition to those usually supplied by a consultant.

7. DUTY TO ALL CONTRACTUAL PARTIES

7.1 The professional engineer shall act with fairness and honesty with his client or employer and any party who engages in a contractual agreement with them.

7.2 He shall co-operate with any parties under contract and make every reasonable effort to facilitate completion of the work in accordance with the terms of the contract.

7.3 He shall act in an impartial manner in dealing with disputes between the contractual parties.

I hereby subscribe to the above code of ethics
to which I set my seal and signature.

.... P. Eng.

Adopted November 1st, 1921.
Rewritten and Adopted, February 28, 1968.

Latest Revision Date Shown 1968. Reprinted by permission of The Association of Professional Engineers of the Province of Manitoba.

ASSOCIATION OF PROFESSIONAL ENGINEERS OF THE PROVINCE OF NEW BRUNSWICK

CANONS OF ETHICS FOR ENGINEERS

FOREWORD

Honesty, justice, and courtesy form a moral philosophy which, associated with mutual interest among men, constitute the foundation of ethics. The engineer should recognize such a standard, not in passive observance, but as a set of dynamic principles guiding his conduct and way of life. It is his duty to practice his profession according to these Canons of Ethics.

As the keystone of professional conduct is integrity, the engineer will discharge his duties with fidelity to the public, his employers, and clients, and with fairness and impartiality to all. It is his duty to interest himself in public welfare, and to be ready to apply his special knowledge for the benefit of mankind. He should uphold the honor and dignity of his profession and also avoid association with any enterprise of questionable character. In his dealings with fellow engineers he should be fair and tolerant.

PROFESSIONAL LIFE

Sec. 1.   The engineer will co-operate in extending the effectiveness of the engineering profession by interchanging information and experience with other engineers and students and by contributing to the work of engineering societies, schools, and the scientific and engineering press.

Sec. 2.   He will not advertise his work or merit in a self-laudatory manner, and he will avoid all conduct or practice likely to discredit or do injury to the dignity and honor of his profession.

RELATIONS WITH THE PUBLIC

Sec. 3.   The engineer will endeavor to extend public knowledge

153

of engineering, and will discourage the spreading of untrue, unfair, and exaggerated statements regarding engineering.

Sec. 4.   He will have due regard for the safety of life and health of the public and employees who may be affected by the work for which he is responsible.

Sec. 5.   He will express an opinion only when it is founded on adequate knowledge and honest conviction while he is serving as a witness before a court, commission, or other tribunal.

Sec. 6.   He will not issue ex parte statements, criticisms, or arguments on matters connected with public policy which are inspired or paid for by private interests, unless he indicates on whose behalf he is making the statement.

Sec. 7.   He will refrain from expressing publicly an opinion on an engineering subject unless he is informed as to the facts relating thereto.

RELATIONS WITH CLIENTS AND EMPLOYERS

Sec. 8.   The Engineer will act in professional matters for each client or employer as a faithful agent or trustee.

Sec. 9.   He will act with fairness and justice between his client or employer and the contractor when dealing with contracts.

Sec. 10.   He will make his status clear to his client or employer before undertaking an engagement if he may be called upon to decide on the use of inventions, apparatus, or any other thing in which he may have a financial interest.

Sec. 11.   He will guard against conditions that are dangerous or threatening to life, limb, or property on work for which he is responsible, or if he is not responsible, will promptly call such conditions to the attention of those who are responsible.

Sec. 12.   He will present clearly the consequences to be expected from deviations proposed if his engineering judgment is overruled by non-technical authority in cases where he is responsible for the technical adequacy of engineering work.

Sec. 13.   He will engage, or advise his client or employer to engage, and he will co-operate with, other experts and specialists whenever the client's or employer's interests are best served by such service.

Sec. 14.   He will disclose no information concerning the business affairs or technical processes of clients or employers without their consent.

Sec. 15.   He will not accept compensation, financial or otherwise, from more than one interested party for the same service, or for services pertaining to the same work, without the consent of all interested parties.

Sec. 16.   He will not accept commissions or allowances, directly or indirectly, from contractors or other parties dealing with his client or employer in connection with work for which he is responsible.

Sec. 17.   He will not be financially interested in the bids as or of a contractor on competitive work for which he is employed as an engineer unless he has the consent of his client or employer.

Sec. 18.   He will promptly disclose to his client or employer any interest in a business which may compete with or affect the business of his client or employer. He will not allow an interest in any business to affect his decision regarding engineering work for which he is employed, or which he may be called upon to perform.

RELATIONS WITH ENGINEERS

Sec. 19.   The engineer will endeavor to protect the engineering profession collectively and individually from misrepresentation and misunderstanding.

Sec. 20.   He will take care that credit for engineering work is given to those to whom credit is properly due.

Sec. 21.   He will uphold the principle of appropriate and adequate compensation for those engaged in engineering work, including those in subordinate capacities, as being in the public interest and maintaining the standards of the profession.

Sec. 22.   He will endeavor to provide opportunity for the professional development and advancement of engineers in his employ.

Sec. 23.   He will not directly or indirectly injure the professional reputation, prospects, or practice of another engineer. However, if he considers that an engineer is guilty of unethical, illegal, or unfair practice, he will present the information to the proper authority for action.

Sec. 24.   He will exercise due restraint in criticizing another engineer's work in public, recognizing the fact that the engineering societies and the engineering press provide the proper forum for technical discussions and criticism.

Sec. 25.   He will not try to supplant another engineer in a particular employment after becoming aware that definite steps have been taken toward the other's employment.

Sec. 26.   He will not compete with another engineer on the basis of charges for work by underbidding, through reducing his normal fees after having been informed of the charges named by the other.

Sec. 27.   He will not use the advantages of a salaried position to compete unfairly with another engineer.

Sec. 28.   He will not become associated in responsibility for work with engineers who do not conform to ethical practices.

Latest Revision Date Shown 1982.

ASSOCIATION OF PROFESSIONAL ENGINEERS OF THE PROVINCE OF NEWFOUNDLAND

CODE OF PROFESSIONAL ETHICS

GENERAL

1. A professional engineer owes certain duties to the public, his employers, to other members of his profession and to himself and shall act at all times with:
   (a) fairness and loyalty to his associates, employers, subordinates and employees;
   (b) fidelity to public needs; and
   (c) devotion to high ideals of personal honour and professional integrity.

DUTY OF PROFESSIONAL ENGINEER TO THE PUBLIC

2. A professional engineer shall,
   (a) endeavour at all times to enhance the public regard for his profession by extending the public knowledge thereof and discouraging untrue, unfair or exaggerated statements with respect to professional engineering;
   (b) not give opinions or make statements on professional engineering projects of public interest that are inspired or paid for by private interests unless he clearly discloses on whose behalf he is giving the opinions or making the statements;
   (c) not express publicly or while he is serving as a witness before a court, commission or other tribunal opinions on professional engineering matters that are not founded on adequate knowledge and honest conviction;
   (d) make effective provisions for the safety of life and health of a person who may be affected by the work for which he is responsible; and,
   (e) sign or seal only those plans, specifications and reports actually made by him or under his personal supervision and direction.

DUTY OF PROFESSIONAL ENGINEER TO EMPLOYER

3. A professional engineer shall,
   (a) act in professional engineering matters for each employer as a faithful agent or trustee and shall regard as confidential any information obtained by him as to the business affairs, technical methods or processes of an employer;
   (b) present clearly to his employers the consequences to be expected from any deviation proposed in the work if his professional engineering judgment is overruled by non-technical authority in cases where he is responsible for the technical adequacy of professional engineering work;
   (c) have no interest, direct or indirect, in any materials, supplies or equipment used by his employer or in any person or firms receiving contracts from his employer unless he informs his employer in advance of the nature of the interest;
   (d) not tender on competitive work upon which he may be acting as a professional engineer unless he first advises his employer;
   (e) not act as consulting engineer in respect of any work upon which he may be the contractor unless he first advises his employer; and,
   (f) not accept compensation, financial or otherwise, for a particular service, from more than one person except with the full knowledge of all interested parties.

DUTY OF PROFESSIONAL ENGINEER TO OTHER PROFESSIONAL ENGINEERS

4. A professional engineer shall,
   (a) conduct himself towards other professional engineers with courtesy and good faith;
   (b) not accept any engagement to review the work of another professional engineer for the same employer except with the knowledge of that engineer, or except where the connection of that engineer with the work has been terminated;
   (c) not maliciously injure the reputation or business of another professional engineer;
   (d) not attempt to gain an advantage over other members of

his profession by paying or accepting a commission in securing professional engineering work; and,

(e) not advertise in a misleading manner or in a manner injurious to the dignity of his profession, but shall seek to advertise by establishing a well-merited reputation for personal capacity.

DUTY OF PROFESSIONAL ENGINEER TO HIMSELF

5. A professional engineer shall,
   (a) maintain the honour and integrity of his profession and without fear or favour expose before the proper tribunals unprofessional or dishonest conduct by any other member of the profession; and,
   (b) undertake only such work as he is competent to perform by virtue of his training and experience, and shall, where advisable, retain and co-operate with other professional engineers or specialists.

Latest Revision Date Not Shown.

THE ASSOCIATION OF PROFESSIONAL ENGINEERS, GEOLOGISTS AND GEOPHYSICISTS OF THE NORTHWEST TERRITORIES

CODE OF ETHICS

1. A Professional Engineer, Geologist or Geophysicist shall recognize that professional ethics is founded upon integrity, competence and devotion to service and to the advancement of human welfare, with due respect to the total environment. This concept shall guide his conduct at all times.

DUTIES OF THE PROFESSIONAL ENGINEER, GEOLOGIST, OR GEOPHYSICIST TO THE PUBLIC

A Professional Engineer, Geologist or Geophysicist:

2. shall have proper regard in all his work for the safety, health and welfare of the public;
3. shall endeavour to extend public understanding of engineering, geology and geophysics and their places in society;
4. shall, where his professional knowledge may benefit the public, seek opportunities to serve in public affairs;
5. shall not be associated with enterprises contrary to the public interest or sponsored by persons of questionable integrity;
6. shall undertake only such work as he is competent to perform by virtue of his training and experience;
7. shall sign and seal only such plans, documents or work as he himself has prepared or carried out or as have been prepared or carried out under his direct professional supervision;
8. shall express opinions on engineering, geological or geophysical matters only on the basis of adequate knowledge and honest conviction.

DUTIES OF THE PROFESSIONAL ENGINEER, GEOLOGIST, OR GEOPHYSICIST TO HIS CLIENT OR EMPLOYER

A Professional Engineer, Geologist or Geophysicist:

9. shall act for his client or employer as a faithful agent or trustee;
10. shall not accept remuneration for services rendered other than from his client or his employer;
11. shall not disclose confidential information without the consent of his client or employer;
12. shall not undertake any assignment which may create a conflict of interest with his client or employer without the full knowledge of the client or employer;
13. shall present clearly to his clients or employers the consequences to be expected if his professional judgment is overruled by other authorities in matters pertaining to work for which he is professionally responsible.

DUTIES OF THE PROFESSIONAL ENGINEER, GEOLOGIST OR GEOPHYSICIST TO THE PROFESSION

A Professional Engineer, Geologist or Geophysicist:
14. shall endeavour at all times to improve the competence, dignity and prestige of his profession;
15. shall conduct himself towards other professional engineers, geologists and geophysicists with fairness and good faith;
16. shall not advertise his professional services in self-laudatory language or in any other manner derogatory to the dignity of his professions;
17. shall not attempt to supplant another engineer, geologist or geophysicist in an engagement after definite steps have been taken toward the other's employment;
18. shall not use the advantages of a salaried position to compete unfairly with another engineer, geologist or geophysicist;
19. shall not exert undue influence or offer, solicit or accept compensation for the purpose of affecting negotiations for an engagement;
20. shall not invite or submit proposals under conditions that constitute price competition for professional services;
21. shall advise the Council of the Association of any practice by another member of his profession which he believes to be contrary to this Code of Ethics.

Latest Revision Date Not Shown.

ASSOCIATION OF PROFESSIONAL ENGINEERS OF NOVA SCOTIA

CANONS OF ETHICS FOR ENGINEERS

GENERAL

1 A professional Engineer shall recognize that professional ethics are founded upon integrity, competence and devotion to service and to the advancement of public welfare. This concept shall guide his conduct at all times.

RELATIONS WITH THE PUBLIC

A Professional Engineer:

2 shall regard his duty to public welfare as paramount.

3 shall endeavor to enhance the public regard for his profession by extending the public knowledge thereof.

4 shall undertake only such work as he is competent to perform by virtue of his training and experience.

5 shall sign and seal only such plans, documents or work as he himself has prepared or carried out or as have been prepared or carried out under his direct professional supervision.

6 shall express opinions on engineering matters only on the basis of adequate knowledge, competence and honest conviction.

7 shall express opinions or make statements on engineering projects of public interest that are inspired or paid for by private interest only if he clearly discloses on whose behalf he is giving the opinion or making the statements.

8 shall not be associated with enterprises contrary to public interest or sponsored by persons of questionable integrity.

RELATIONS WITH CLIENTS AND EMPLOYERS

A Professional Engineer:

9 shall act for his client or employer as a faithful agent or

trustee and shall act with fairness and justice between his client or employer and the contractor when contracts are involved.

10 shall not accept compensation, financial or otherwise, from more than one interested party for the same service, or for service pertaining to the same work, without the consent of all interested parties.

11 shall not disclose confidential information without the consent of his client or employer.

12 shall not be financially interested in bids on competitive work for which he is employed as an engineer unless he has the consent of his client or employer.

13 shall not undertake any assignment which may create a conflict of interest with his client or employer without the full knowledge of the client or employer.

14 shall present clearly to his clients or employers the consequences to be expected if his professional judgment is overruled by other authorities in matters pertaining to work for which he is professionally responsible.

15 shall refrain from unprofessional conduct or from actions which he considers to be contrary to the public good, even if expected or directed by his employer or client, to act in such a manner.

16 shall not expect or direct an employee or subordinate to act in a manner that he or the employee or subordinate considers to be unprofessional or contrary to the public good.

17 shall guard against conditions that are dangerous or threatening to life, limb or property on work for which he is responsible, or if he is not responsible, will promptly call such conditions to the attention of those who are responsible.

RELATIONS WITH THE PROFESSION

A Professional Engineer:

18 shall co-operate in extending the effectiveness of the engineering profession by interchanging information and experience with other engineers and students and by contributing to the work of engineering societies, schools and the scientific and engineering press.

19 shall endeavour at all times to improve the competence, and thus the dignity and prestige of his profession.

20 shall not advertise his work on merit in a self-laudatory man-

ner and shall avoid all conduct or practice likely to discredit or do injury to the dignity and honor of his profession.

21 shall not attempt to supplant another engineer in an engagement after a definite commitment has been made toward the other's employment.

22 shall not exert undue influence or offer, solicit or accept compensation for the purpose of affecting negotiations for an engagement.

23 shall not compete with another engineer on the basis of charges for work by underbidding, through reducing his normal fees after having been informed of the charges named by the other.

24 shall not use the advantages of a salaried position to compete unfairly with another engineer.

25 shall advise the Discipline Committee of any practice by another member of his profession which he believes to be contrary to this Code of Ethics.

26 shall take care that credit for engineering work is given to those to whom credit is properly due.

27 shall uphold the principle of appropriate and adequate compensation for those engaged in engineering work including those in subordinate capacities as being in the public interest maintaining the standards of the profession.

28 shall endeavor to provide opportunity for the professional development and advancement of engineers in his employ.

Latest Revision Date Shown 1952.

ASSOCIATION OF PROFESSIONAL ENGINEERS OF ONTARIO

CODE OF ETHICS   REVISED APRIL 1977

GENERAL

1. A professional engineer owes certain duties to the public, to his employers, to his clients, to other members of his profession, and to himself, and shall act at all times with:
   (a) fairness and loyalty to his associates, employers, clients, subordinates and employees;
   (b) fidelity to public needs; and
   (c) devotion to high ideals of personal honour and professional integrity.

DUTY OF PROFESSIONAL ENGINEER TO THE PUBLIC

2. A professional engineer shall:
   (a) regard his duty to public welfare as paramount;
   (b) endeavour at all times to enhance the public regard for his profession by extending the public knowledge thereof and discouraging untrue, unfair or exaggerated statements with respect to professional engineering;
   (c) not give opinions or make statements on professional engineering projects of public interest that are inspired or paid for by private interests unless he clearly discloses on whose behalf he is giving the opinions or making the statements;
   (d) not express publicly, or while he is serving as a witness before a court, commission or other tribunal, opinions on professional engineering matters that are not founded on adequate knowledge and honest conviction;
   (e) make effective provisions for the safety of life and health of a person who may be affected by the work for which he is responsible; and at all times shall act to correct or report any situation which he feels may endanger the safety or the welfare of the public;
   (f) make effective provision for meeting lawful standards, rules, or regulations relating to environmental control and

165

protection, in connection with any work being undertaken by him or under his responsibility; and

(g) sign or seal only those plans, specifications and reports actually made by him or under his personal supervision and direction.

DUTY OF PROFESSIONAL ENGINEER TO EMPLOYER

3. A professional engineer shall:
   (a) act in professional engineering matters for each employer as a faithful agent or trustee and shall regard as confidential any information obtained by him as to the business affairs, technical methods or processes of an employer and avoid or disclose any conflict of interest which might influence his actions or judgement;
   (b) present clearly to his employers the consequences to be expected from any deviations proposed in the work if his professional engineering judgement is overruled by non-technical authority in cases where he is responsible for the technical adequacy of professional engineering work;
   (c) have no interest, direct or indirect, in any materials, supplies or equipment used by his employer or in any persons or firms receiving contracts from his employer unless he informs his employer in advance of the nature of the interest;
   (d) not tender on competitive work upon which he may be acting as a professional engineer unless he first advises his employer;
   (e) not act as consulting engineer in respect of any work upon which he may be the contractor unless he first advises his employer; and
   (f) not accept compensation, financial or otherwise, for a particular service, from more than one person except with the full knowledge of all interested parties.

DUTY OF PROFESSIONAL ENGINEER IN INDEPENDENT PRACTICE TO CLIENT

4. A professional engineer in private practice, in addition to all other sections, shall:

   (a) disclose immediately any interest, direct or indirect, which might in any way be construed as prejudicial to his professional judgement in rendering service to his client;

   (b) if he is an employee-engineer and is contracting in his own name to perform professional engineering work for other than his employer, provide his client with a written statement of the nature of his status as an employee and the attendant limitations on his services to the client. In addition he shall satisfy himself that such work will not conflict with his duty to his employer;

   (c) carry out his work in accordance with applicable statutes, regulations, standards, codes, and by-laws; and

   (d) co-operate as necessary in working with such other professionals as may be engaged on a project.

DUTY OF PROFESSIONAL ENGINEER TO OTHER PROFESSIONAL ENGINEERS

5. A professional engineer shall:

   (a) conduct himself towards other professional engineers with courtesy and good faith;

   (b) not accept any engagement to review the work of another professional engineer for the same employer except with the knowledge of that engineer, or except where the connection of that engineer with the work has been terminated;

   (c) not maliciously injure the reputation or business of another professional engineer;

   (d) not attempt to gain an advantage over other members of his profession by paying or accepting a commission in securing professional engineering work;

   (e) not advertise in a misleading manner or in a manner injurious to the dignity of his profession, but shall seek to advertise by establishing a well-merited reputation for personal capability; and

   (f) give proper credit for engineering work, uphold the principle of adequate compensation for engineering work, provide opportunity for professional development and advancement of his associates and subordinates; and extend the effectiveness of the profession through the interchange of engineering information and experience.

DUTY OF PROFESSIONAL ENGINEER TO HIMSELF

6. A professional engineer shall:
   (a) maintain the honour and integrity of his profession and without fear or favour expose before the proper tribunals unprofessional or dishonest conduct by any other members of the profession; and
   (b) undertake only such work as he is competent to perform by virtue of his training and experience, and shall, where advisable, retain and co-operate with other professional engineers or specialists.

Latest Revision Date Shown 1977.

ASSOCIATION OF PROFESSIONAL ENGINEERS OF THE PROVINCE OF PRINCE EDWARD ISLAND

CODE OF ETHICS FOR ENGINEERS

FOREWORD

Honesty, justice and courtesy form a moral philosophy which, associated with mutual interest among men, constitutes the foundation of ethics. The engineer should recognize such a standard, not in passive observance, but as a set of dynamic principles guiding his conduct and way of life. It is his duty to practice his profession according to these Canons of Ethics.

As the keystone of professional conduct is integrity the engineer will discharge his duties with fidelity to the public, his employers and clients, and with fairness and impartiality to all. It is his duty to interest himself in public welfare, and to be ready to apply his special knowledge for the benefit of mankind. He should uphold the honor and dignity of his profession and avoid association with any enterprise of questionable character. In his dealings with fellow engineers he should be fair and tolerant.

PROFESSIONAL LIFE

Sec. 1.   The engineer will cooperate in extending the effectiveness of the engineering profession by interchanging information and experience with other engineers and students and by contributing to the work of engineering societies, schools and the scientific and engineering press.

Sec. 2.   He will not advertise his work or merit in a self-laudatory manner, and he will avoid all conduct or practice likely to discredit or do injury to the dignity and honor of his profession.

RELATIONS WITH THE PUBLIC

Sec. 3.   The engineer will endeavour to extend public knowl-

169

edge of engineering, and will discourage the spreading of untrue, unfair and exaggerated statements regarding engineering.

Sec. 4. He will have due regard for the safety of life and health of public and employees who may be affected by the work for which he is responsible.

Sec. 5. He will express an opinion only when it is founded on adequate knowledge and honest conviction while he is serving as a witness before a court, commission or other tribunal.

Sec. 6. He will not issue ex parte statements, criticisms or arguments on matters connected with public policy which are inspired or paid for by private interests, unless he indicates on whose behalf he is making the statement.

Sec. 7. He will refrain from expressing publicly an opinion on an engineering subject unless he is informed as to the facts relating thereto.

RELATIONS WITH CLIENTS AND EMPLOYERS

Sec. 8. The engineer will act in professional matters for each client or employer as a faithful agent or trustee.

Sec. 9. He will act with fairness and justice between his client or employer and the contractor when dealing with contracts.

Sec. 10. He will make his status clear to his client or employer before undertaking an engagement if he may be called upon to decide on the use of inventions, apparatus, or any other thing in which he may have a financial interest.

Sec. 11. He will guard against conditions that are dangerous or threatening to life, limb or property on work for which he is responsible, or if he is not responsible, will promptly call such conditions to the attention of those who are responsible.

Sec. 12. He will present clearly the consequences to be expected from deviations proposed if his engineering judgment is overruled by non-technical authority in cases where he is responsible for the technical adequacy of engineering work.

Sec. 13. He will engage or advise his client or employer to engage, and he will cooperate with, other experts and specialists whenever the client's or employer's interests are best served by such service.

Sec. 14. He will disclose no information concerning the business affairs or technical process of clients or employers without their consent.

170

Sec. 15. He will not accept compensation, financial or otherwise, from more than one interested party for the same service, or for services pertaining to the same work, without the consent of all interested parties.

Sec. 16.   He will not accept commissions or allowances, directly or indirectly, from contractors or other parties dealing with his client or employer in connection with work for which he is responsible.

Sec. 17.   He will not be financially interested in the bids as or of a contractor on competitive work for which he is employed as an engineer unless he has the consent of his client or employer.

Sec. 18.   He will promptly disclose to his client or employer any interest in a business which may compete with or affect the business of his client or employer. He will not allow an interest in any business to affect his decision regarding engineering work for which he is employed, or which he may be called upon to perform.

RELATIONS WITH ENGINEERS

Sec. 19.   The engineer will endeavour to protect the engineering profession collectively and individually from misrepresentation and misunderstanding.

Sec. 20.   He will take care that credit for engineering work is given to those to whom credit is properly due.

Sec. 21.   He will uphold the principle of appropriate and adequate compensation for those engaged in engineering work, including those in subordinate capacities, as being in the public interest and maintaining the standards of the profession.

Sec. 22.   He will endeavour to provide opportunity for the professional development and advancement of engineers in his employ.

Sec. 23.   He will not directly or indirectly injure the professional reputation, prospects or practice of another engineer. However, if he considers that an engineer is guilty of unethical, illegal or unfair practice, he will present the information to the proper authority for action.

Sec. 24.   He will exercise due restraint in criticizing another engineer's work in public, recognizing the fact that the engineering societies and the engineering press provide the proper forum for technical discussions and criticism.

Sec. 25.   He will not try to supplant another engineer in a particular employment after becoming aware that definite steps have been taken toward the other's employment.

Sec. 26.   He will not compete with another engineer on the basis of charges for work by underbidding, through reducing his normal fees after having been informed of the charges named by the other.

Sec. 27.   He will not use the advantages of a salaried position to compete unfairly with another engineer.

Sec. 28.   He will not become associated in responsibility for work with engineers who do not conform to ethical practices.

Latest Revision Date Shown 1955.
Reprinted by permission of A.P.E.P.E.I.

ORDRE DES INGÉNIEURS DU QUÉBEC

CODE DE DÉONTOLOGIE DES INGÉNIEURS

SECTION I
DISPOSITIONS GÉNÉRALES

1.01. Le présent règlement est adopté en vertu de l'article 87 du Code des professions (L.R.Q., c. C-26).

1.02. Dans le présent règlement, à moins que le contexte n'indique un sens différent, le mot "client" signifie celui qui bénéficie des services professionnels d'un ingénieur, y compris un employeur.

1.03. La Loi d'interprétation (L.R.Q., c. I-16), avec ses modifications présentes et futures, s'applique au présent règlement.

SECTION II
DEVOIRS ET OBLIGATIONS ENVERS LE PUBLIC

2.01. Dans tous les aspects de son travail, l'ingénieur doit respecter ses obligations envers l'homme et tenir compte des conséquences de l'exécution de ses travaux sur l'environnement et sur la vie, la santé et la propriété de toute personne.

2.02. L'ingénieur doit appuyer toute mesure susceptible d'améliorer la qualité et la disponibilité de ses services professionnels.

2.03. L'ingénieur doit, lorsqu'il considère que des travaux sont dangereux pour la sécurité publique, en informer l'Ordre des ingénieurs du Québec ou les responsables de tels travaux.

2.04. L'ingénieur ne doit exprimer son avis sur des questions ayant trait à l'ingénierie, que si cet avis est basé sur des connaissances suffisantes et sur d'honnêtes convictions.

2.05. L'ingénieur doit favoriser les mesures d'éducation et d'information dans le domaine où il exerce.

SECTION III
DEVOIRS ET OBLIGATIONS ENVERS LE CLIENT
§ 1. DISPOSITIONS GÉNÉRALES

3.01.01. Avant d'accepter un mandat, l'ingénieur doit tenir   173 compte des limites de ses connaissances et de ses aptitudes ainsi que des moyens dont il peut disposer pour l'exécuter.

3.01.02. L'ingénieur doit reconnaître en tout temps le droit du client de consulter un autre ingénieur. S'il y va de l'intérêt du client, l'ingénieur retient les services d'experts après en avoir informé son client, ou avise ce dernier de le faire.

3.01.03. L'ingénieur doit s'abstenir d'exercer dans des conditions ou des états susceptibles de compromettre la qualité de ses services.

---

§ 2. INTÉGRITÉ

3.02.01. L'ingénieur doit s'acquitter de ses obligations professionnelles avec intégrité.

3.02.02. L'ingénieur doit éviter toute fausse représentation concernant sa compétence ou l'efficacité de ses propres services et de ceux généralement assurés par les membres de sa profession.

3.02.03. L'ingénieur doit, dès que possible, informer son client de l'ampleur et des modalités du mandat que ce dernier lui a confié et obtenir son accord à ce sujet.

3.02.04. L'ingénieur doit s'abstenir d'exprimer des avis ou de donner des conseils contradictoires ou incomplets et de présenter ou utiliser des plans, devis et autres documents qu'il sait ambigüs ou qui ne sont pas suffisamment explicites.

3.02.05. L'ingénieur doit informer le plus tôt possible son client de toute erreur préjudiciable et difficilement réparable qu'il a commise dans l'exécution de son mandat.

3.02.06. L'ingénieur doit apporter un soin raisonnable aux biens confiés à sa garde par un client et il ne peut prêter ou utiliser ceux-ci à des fins autres que celles pour lesquelles ils lui ont été confiés.

3.02.07. Si on écarte un avis de l'ingénieur dans le cas où celui-ci est responsable de la qualité technique de travaux d'ingéniérie, l'ingénieur doit indiquer clairement à son client, par écrit, les conséquences qui peuvent en découler.

3.02.08. L'ingénieur ne doit pas recourir à des procédés malhonnêtes ou douteux dans l'exercice de ses activités professionnelles.

3.02.09. L'ingénieur doit s'abstenir de verser ou de s'engager à verser, directement ou indirectement, tout avantage, ristourne ou commission en vue d'obtenir un contrat ou lors de l'exécution de travaux d'ingéniérie.

3.02.10. L'ingénieur doit faire preuve d'impartialité dans ses rapports entre son client et les entrepreneurs, fournisseurs et autres personnes faisant affaires avec son client.

§ 3. DISPONIBILITÉ ET DILIGENCE

3.03.01. L'ingénieur doit faire preuve, dans l'exercice de sa profession, d'une disponibilité et d'une diligence raisonnables.

3.03.02. L'ingénieur doit en plus des avis et des conseils, fournir à son client les explications nécessaires à la compréhension et à l'appréciation des services qu'il lui rend.

3.03.03. L'ingénieur doit rendre compte à son client lorsque celui-ci le requiert.

3.03.04. L'ingénieur ne peut, sauf pour un motif juste et raisonnable, cesser d'agir pour le compte d'un client. Constituent notamment des motifs justes et raisonnables:

a) le fait que l'ingénieur soit en situation de conflit d'intérêts ou dans un contexte tel que son indépendance professionnelle puisse être mise en doute;

b) l'incitation, de la part du client, à l'accomplissement d'actes illégaux, injustes ou frauduleux;

c) le fait que le client ignore les avis de l'ingénieur.

3.03.05. Avant de cesser d'exercer ses fonctions pour le compte d'un client, l'ingénieur doit lui faire parvenir un préavis de délaissement dans un délai raisonnable.

§ 4. RESPONSABILITÉ

3.04.01. L'ingénieur doit apposer son sceau et sa signature sur l'original et les copies de chaque plans, devis, rapport technique, étude, cahier des charges et autres documents d'ingénierie qu'il a préparés lui-même ou qui ont été préparés sous sa direction et surveillance immédiates par des personnes qui ne sont pas membres de l'Ordre.

L'ingénieur peut également apposer son sceau et sa signature sur l'original et les copies des documents prévus au présent article qui ont été préparés, signés et scellés par un autre ingénieur.

L'ingénieur ne doit ou ne peut apposer son sceau et sa signature que dans les seuls cas prévus au présent article.

§ 5. INDÉPENDANCE ET DÉSINTÉRESSEMENT

3.05.01. L'ingénieur doit, dans l'exercice de sa profession, subordonner son intérêt personnel à celui de son client.

3.05.02. L'ingénieur doit ignorer toute intervention d'un tiers qui pourrait influer sur l'exécution de ses devoirs professionnels au préjudice de son client.

Sans restreindre la généralité de ce qui précède, l'ingénieur ne doit accepter, directement ou indirectement, aucun avantage ou ristourne en argent ou autrement, d'un fournisseur de marchandises ou de services relativement à des travaux d'ingénierie qu'il effectue pour le compte d'un client.

3.05.03. L'ingénieur doit sauvegarder en tout temps son indépendance professionnelle et éviter toute situation où il serait en conflit d'intérêts.

3.05.04. Dès qu'il constate qu'il se trouve dans une situation de conflit d'intérêts, l'ingénieurs doit en aviser son client et lui demander s'il l'autorise à poursuivre son mandat.

3.05.05. L'ingénieur ne peut partager ses honoraires qu'avec un confrère et dans la mesure où ce partage correspond à une répartition des services et des responsabilités.

3.05.06. L'ingénieur ne doit généralement agir, dans l'exécution d'un mandat, que pour l'une des parties en cause, soit son client. Toutefois, si ses devoirs professionnels exigent qu'il agisse autrement, l'ingénieur doit en informer son client. Il ne doit accepter le versement de ses honoraires que de son client ou du représentant de ce dernier.

§ 6. SECRET PROFESSIONNEL

3.06.01. L'ingénieur doit respecter le secret de tout renseignement de nature confidentielle obtenu dans l'exercice de sa profession.

3.06.02. L'ingénieur ne peut être relevé du secret professionnel qu'avec l'autorisation de son client ou lorsque la loi l'ordonne.

3.06.03. L'ingénieur ne doit pas faire usage de renseignements de nature confidentielle au préjudice d'un client ou en vue d'obtenir directement ou indirectement un avantage pour lui-même ou pour autrui.

3.06.04. L'ingénieur ne doit pas accepter un mandat qui comporte ou peut comporter la révélation ou l'usage de renseignements ou documents confidentiels obtenus d'un autre client, sans le consentement de ce dernier.

§ 7. ACCESSIBILITÉ DES DOSSIERS

3.07.01. L'ingénieur doit respecter le droit de son client de prendre connaissance et d'obtenir copie des documents qui le concernent dans tout dossier qu'il a constitué à son sujet.

§ 8. FIXATION ET PAIEMENT DES HONORAIRES

3.08.01. L'ingénieur doit demander et accepter des honoraires justes et raisonnables.

3.08.02. Les honoraires sont justes et raisonnables s'ils sont justifiés par les circonstances et proportionés aux services rendus. L'ingénieur doit notamment tenir compte des facteurs suivants pour la fixation de ses honoraires:

a) le temps consacré à l'exécution du mandat;

b) la difficulté et l'importance du mandat;

c) la prestation de services inhabituels ou exigeant une compétence ou une célérité exceptionnelles;

d) la responsabilité assumée.

3.08.03. L'ingénieur doit prévenir son client du coût approximatif de ses services et des modalités de paiement. Il doit s'abstenir d'exiger d'avance le paiement de ses honoraires; il peut cependant exiger des avances.

3.08.04. L'ingénieur doit fournir à son client toutes les explications nécessaires à la compréhension de son relevé d'honoraires et des modalités de paiement.

SECTION IV
DEVOIRS ET OBLIGATIONS ENVERS LA PROFESSION
§ 1. ACTES DÉROGATOIRES

4.01.01. En outre des actes dérogatoires mentionnés aux articles 57 et 58 du Code des professions, est dérogatoire à la dignité de la profession le fait pour un ingénieur:

a) de participer ou de contribuer à l'exercice illégal de la profession;

b) d'inciter quelqu'un de façon pressante ou répétée à recourir à ses services professionnels;

c) de communiquer avec la personne qui a porté plainte sans la permission écrite et préalable du syndic ou de son adjoint, lorsqu'il est informé d'une enquête sur sa conduite ou sa compétence professionnelle ou lorsqu'il a reçu signification d'une plainte à son endroit;

d) de refuser de se soumettre à la procédure de conciliation et d'arbitrage des comptes et à la décision des arbitres;

e) de procéder en justice contre un confrère sur une question relative à l'exercice de la profession avant d'avoire demandé la conciliation au président de l'Ordre;

f) de refuser ou de négliger de se rendre au bureau du syndic, de l'un de ses adjoints ou d'un syndic correspondant, sur demande à cet effet par l'un d'eux;

g) de ne pas avertir le syndic sans délai, s'il croit qu'un ingénieur enfreint le présent règlement.

---

§ 2. RELATION AVEC L'ORDRE ET LES CONFRÈRES

4.02.01. L'ingénieur à qui l'Ordre demande de participer à un conseil d'arbitrage de compte, à un comité de discipline ou d'inspection professionnelle, doit accepter cette fonction à moins de motifs exceptionnels.

4.02.02. L'ingénieur doit répondre dans les plus brefs délais à toute correspondance provenant du syndic de l'Ordre, du syndic adjoint ou d'un syndic correspondant, des enquêteurs, des membres du comité d'inspection professionnelle ou du secrétaire de ce dernier comité.

4.02.03. L'ingénieur ne doit pas surprendre la bonne foi d'un confrère, abuser de sa confiance, être déloyal envers lui ou porter malicieusement atteinte à sa réputation. Sans restreindre la généralité de ce qui précède, l'ingénieur ne doit pas notamment:

a) s'attribuer le mérite d'un travail d'ingénierie qui revient à un confrère;

b) profiter de sa qualité d'employeur ou de cadre pour limiter de quelque façon que ce soit l'autonomie professionnelle d'un ingénieur à son emploi ou sous sa responsabilité, notamment à l'égard de l'usage du titre d'ingénieur ou de l'obligation pour tout ingénieur d'engager sa responsabilité professionnelle.

4.02.04. Lorsqu'un client demande à un ingénieur d'examiner ou de réviser des travaux d'ingénierie qu'il n'a pas lui-même exécutés, ce dernier doit en aviser l'ingénieur concerné et, s'il y a lieu, s'assurer que le mandat de son confrère est terminé.

4.02.05. Lorsqu'un ingénieur remplace un confrère dans des travaux d'ingénierie, il doit en avertir ce confrère et s'assurer que le mandat de ce dernier est terminé.

4.02.06. L'ingénieur appelé à collaborer avec un confrère doit préserver son indépendance professionnelle. Si on lui confie une tâche contraire à sa conscience ou à ses principes, il peut demander d'en être dispensé.

§ 3. CONTRIBUTION À L'AVANCEMENT DE LA PROFESSION

4.03.01. L'ingénieur doit, dans la mesure de ses possibilités, aider au développement de sa profession par l'échange de ses connaissances et de son expérience avec ses confrères et les étudiants, et par sa participation, à titre de professeur ou de maître de stage, aux cours de formation continue et aux stages de perfectionnement.

CODE OF ETHICS OF ENGINEERS

DIVISION I
GENERAL PROVISIONS

1.01. This Regulation is made pursuant to section 87 of the Professional Code (R.S.Q., c. C-26).

1.02. In this Regulation, unless the context indicates otherwise, the word ''client'' means a person to whom an engineer provides professional services, including an employer.

1.03. The Interpretation Act (R.S.Q., c. I-16), with present and future amendments, applies to this Regulation.

DIVISION II
DUTIES AND OBLIGATIONS TOWARDS THE PUBLIC

2.01. In all aspects of his work, the engineer must respect his obligations towards man and take into account the consequences of the performance of his work on the environment and on the life, health and property of every person.

2.02. The engineer must support every measure likely to improve the quality and availability of his professional services.

2.03. Whenever an engineer considers that certain works are a danger to public safety, he must notify the Ordre des ingénieurs du Québec (Order) or the persons responsible for such work.

2.04. The engineer shall express his opinion on matters dealing with engineering only if such opinion is based on sufficient knowledge and honest convictions.

2.05. The engineer must promote educational and information measures in the field in which he practises.

DIVISION III
DUTIES AND OBLIGATIONS TOWARDS CLIENTS
§ 1. GENERAL PROVISIONS

3.01.01. Before accepting a mandate, an engineer must bear in mind the extent of his proficiency and aptitudes and also the means at his disposal to carry out the mandate.

3.01.02. An engineer must at all times acknowledge his client's right to consult another engineer. If it is in the client's interest, the engineer shall retain the services of experts after having informed his client thereof, or he shall advise the latter to do so.

3.01.03. An engineer must refrain from practising under conditions or in circumstances which could impair the quality of his services.

§ 2. INTEGRITY

3.02.01. An engineer must fulfil his professional obligations with integrity.

3.02.02. An engineer must avoid any misrepresentation with respect to his level of competence or the efficiency of his own services and of those generally provided by the members of his profession.

3.02.03. An engineer must, as soon as possible, inform his client of the extent and the terms and conditions of the mandate entrusted to him by the latter and obtain his agreement in that respect.

3.02.04. An engineer must refrain from expressing or giving contradictory or incomplete opinions or advice, and from presenting or using plans specifications and other documents which he knows to be ambiguous or which are not sufficiently explicit.

3.02.05. An engineer must inform his client as early as possible of any error that might cause the latter prejudice and which cannot be easily rectified, made by him in the carrying out of his mandate.

3.02.06. An engineer must take reasonable care of the property entrusted to his care by a client and he may not lend or use it for purposes other than those for which it has been entrusted to him.

3.02.07. Where an engineer is responsible for the technical quality of engineering work, and his opinion is ignored, the engineer must clearly indicate to his client, in writing, the consequences which may result therefrom.

3.02.08. The engineer shall not resort to dishonest or doubtful practices in the performance of his professional activities.

3.02.09. An engineer shall not pay or undertake to pay, directly or indirectly, any benefit, rebate or commission in order to obtain a contract or upon the carrying out of engineering work.

3.02.10. An engineer must be impartial in his relations between his client and the contractors, suppliers and other persons doing business with his client.

§ 3. AVAILABILITY AND DILIGENCE

3.03.01. An engineer must show reasonable availability and diligence in the practice of his profession.

3.03.02. In addition to opinion and counsel, the engineer must furnish his client with any explanations necessary to the understanding and appreciation of the services he is providing him.

3.03.03. An engineer must give an accounting to his client when so requested by the latter.

3.03.04. An engineer may not cease to act for the account of a client unless he has just and reasonable grounds for so doing. The following shall, in particular, constitute just and reasonable grounds:

(*a*) the fact that the engineer is placed in a situation of conflict of interest or in a circumstance whereby his professional independence could be called in question;

(*b*) inducement by the client to illegal, unfair or fraudulent acts;

(*c*) the fact that the client ignores the engineer's advice.

3.03.05. Before ceasing to exercise his functions for the account of a client, the engineer must give advance notice of withdrawal within a reasonable time.

§ 4. RESPONSIBILITY

3.04.01. An engineer must affix his seal and signature on the original and the copies of every plan, specification, technical report, survey, contract specification and other engineering documents prepared by himself or prepared under his immediate control and supervision by persons who are not members of the Order.

An engineer may also affix his seal and signature on the original and the copies of documents mentioned in this section which have been prepared, signed and sealed by another engineer.

An engineer must not affix his seal and signature except in the cases provided for in this section.

---

§ 5. INDEPENDENCE AND IMPARTIALITY

3.05.01. An engineer must, in the practice of his profession, subordinate his personal interest to that of his client.

3.05.02. An engineer must ignore any intervention by a third party which could influence the performance of his professional duties to the detriment of his client.

Without restricting the generality of the foregoing, an engineer shall not accept, directly or indirectly, any benefit or rebate in money or otherwise from a supplier of goods or services relative to engineering work which he performs for the account of a client.

3.05.03. An engineer must safeguard his professional independence at all times and avoid any situation which would put him in conflict of interest.

3.05.04. As soon as he ascertains that he is in a situation of conflict of interest, the engineer must notify his client thereof and ask his authorization to continue his mandate.

3.05.05. An engineer shall share his fees only with a colleague and to the extent where such sharing corresponds to a distribution of services and responsibilities.

3.05.06. In carrying out a mandate, the engineer shall generally act only for one of the parties concerned, namely, his client. However, where his professional duties require that he act otherwise, the engineer must notify his client thereof. He shall accept the payment of his fees only from his client or the latter's representative.

---

§ 6. PROFESSIONAL SECRECY

3.06.01. An engineer must respect the secrecy of all confidential information obtained in the practice of his profession.

3.06.02. An engineer shall be released from professional secrecy only with the authorization of his client or whenever so ordered by law.

3.06.03. An engineer shall not make use of confidential information to the prejudice of a client or with a view to deriving, directly or indirectly, an advantage for himself or for another person.

3.06.04. An engineer shall not accept a mandate which entails or may entail the disclosure or use of confidential information or documents obtained from another client without the latter's consent.

§ 7. ACCESSIBILITY OF RECORDS

3.07.01. An engineer must respect the right of his client to take cognizance of and to obtain copies of the documents that concern the latter in any record which the engineer has made regarding that client.

§ 8. DETERMINATION AND PAYMENT OF FEES

3.08.01. An engineer must charge and accept fair and reasonable fees.

3.08.02. Fees are considered fair and reasonable when they are justified by the circumstances and correspond to the services rendered. In determining his fees, the engineer must, in particular, take the following factors into account:

(*a*) the time devoted to the carrying out of the mandate;

(*b*) the difficulty and magnitude of the mandate;

(*c*) the performance of unusual services or services requiring exceptional competence or speed:

(*d*) the responsibility assumed.

3.08.03. An engineer must inform his client of the approximate cost of his services and of the terms and conditions of payment. He must refrain from demanding advance payment of his fees; he may, however, demand payment on account.

3.08.04. An engineer must give his client all the necessary explanations for the understanding of his statement of fees and the terms and conditions of its payment.

DIVISION IV
DUTIES AND OBLIGATIONS TOWARDS THE
PROFESSION
§ 1. DEROGATORY ACTS

4.01.01. In addition to those referred to in sections 57 and 58 of the Professional Code, the following acts are derogatory to the dignity of the profession:

(*a*) participating or contributing to the illegal practice of the profession;

(*b*) pressing or repeated inducement to make use of his professional services;

(*c*) communicating with the person who lodged a complaint, without the prior written permission of the syndic or his assistant, whenever he is informed of an inquiry into his professional conduct or competence or whenever a complaint has been laid against him;

(*d*) refusing to comply with the procedures for the conciliation and arbitration of accounts and with the arbitrators' award;

(*e*) taking legal action against a colleague on a matter relative to the practice of the profession before applying for conciliation to the president of the Order;

(*f*) refusing or failing to present himself at the office of the syndic, of one of his assistants or of a corresponding syndic, upon request to that effect by one of those persons;

(*g*) not notifying the syndic without delay if he believes that an engineer infringes this Regulation.

§ 2. RELATIONS WITH THE ORDER AND COLLEAGUES

4.02.01. An engineer whose participation in a council for the arbitration of accounts, a committee on discipline or a professional inspection committee is requested by the Order, must accept this duty unless he has exceptional grounds for refusing.

4.02.02. An engineer must, within the shortest delay, answer all correspondence addressed to him by the syndic of the Order, the assistant syndic or a corresponding syndic, investigators or members of the professional inspection committee or the secretary of the said committee.

4.02.03. An engineer shall not abuse a colleague's good faith, be guilty of breach of trust or be disloyal towards him or willfully damage his reputation. Without restricting the generality of the foregoing, the engineer shall not, in particular:

(*a*) take upon himself the credit for engineering work which belongs to a colleague;

(*b*) take advantage of his capacity of employer or executive to limit in any way whatsoever the professional autonomy of an engineer employed by him or under his responsibility, in

185

particular with respect to the use of the title of engineer or the obligation of every engineer to be true to his professional responsibility.

4.02.04. Where a client requests an engineer to examine or review engineering work that he has not peformed himself, the latter must notify the engineer concerned thereof and, where applicable, ensure that the mandate of his colleague has terminated.

4.02.05. Where an engineer replaces a colleague in engineering work, he must notify that colleague thereof and make sure that the latter's mandate has terminated.

4.02.06. An engineer who is called upon to collaborate with a colleague must retain his professional independence. If a task is entrusted to him and such task goes against his conscience or his principles, he may ask to be excused from doing it.

§ 3. CONTRIBUTION TO THE ADVANCEMENT OF THE PROFESSION

4.03.01. An engineer must, as far as he is able, contribute to the development of his profession by sharing his knowledge and experience with his colleagues and students, and by his participation as professor or tutor in continuing training periods and refresher training courses.

Latest Revision Date 1983.

ASSOCIATION OF PROFESSIONAL ENGINEERS OF THE PROVINCE OF SASKATCHEWAN

CODE OF ETHICS

For the governance of the conduct of the members and licensees of the Association, the following Code of Ethics is hereby established:

PREAMBLE

Honesty, justice, and courtesy form a moral philosophy which, associated with mutual interest among men, constitute the foundation of ethics. The Professional Engineer should recognize such a standard, not in passive observance but as a set of dynamic principles guiding his conduct and way of life. It is his duty to practise his profession according to this Code of Ethics.

GENERAL

1. A professional engineer owes certain duties to the public, his employers, other members of his profession and to himself and shall act at all times with,
   (a) fidelity to public needs;
   (b) fairness and loyalty to his associates, employers, subordinates and employees; and
   (c) devotion to high ideals of personal honour and professional integrity.

DUTY OF PROFESSIONAL ENGINEER TO THE PUBLIC

2. A professional engineer shall,
   (a) regard his duty to the public as paramount;
   (b) endeavour to maintain public regard for his profession by discouraging untrue, unfair or exaggerated statements with respect to professional engineering;

187

(c) not give opinions or make statements on professional engineering projects of public interest that are inspired or paid for by private interests unless he clearly discloses on whose behalf he is giving the opinions or making the statements;

(d) not express publicly or while he is serving as a witness before a court, commission or other tribunal, opinions on professional engineering matters that are not founded on adequate knowledge and honest conviction;

(e) make effective provisions for the safety of life and health of a person who may be affected by the work for which he is responsible; and shall act to correct or report any situation which he feels may endanger the public;

(f) not knowingly associate with, or allow the use of his name by, an enterprise of doubtful character, nor shall he sanction the use of his reports, in part or in whole, in a manner calculated to mislead, and if it comes to his knowledge they have been so used, shall take immediate steps to correct any false impression given by them;

(g) on all occasions sign or seal reports, plans and specifications which legally requires sealing and for which he is professionally responsible;

(h) not offer his services for a fee without first notifying the council of the Association of his intent to do so and of the area of speciality in which he proposes to practise, and receiving from the council of the Association permission to do so.

DUTY OF PROFESSIONAL ENGINEER TO EMPLOYER

3. A professional engineer shall,

(a) act for his employer as a faithful agent or trustee and shall regard as confidential any information obtained by him as to the business affairs, technical methods or processes of his employer, and avoid or disclose any conflict of interest which might influence his actions or judgement;

(b) present clearly to his employers the consequences to be expected from any deviations proposed in the work if his professional engineering judgement is overruled in cases where he is responsible for the technical adequacy of professional engineering work;

(c) advise his employer to engage experts and specialists whenever the employer's interests are best served by so doing;

(d) have no interest, direct or indirect in any materials, supplies or equipment used by his employer or in any persons or firms receiving contracts from his employer unless he informs his employer in advance of the nature of the interest;

(e) not act as consulting engineer in respect of any work upon which he may be the contractor unless he first advises his employer; and

(f) not accept compensation, financial or otherwise, for a particular service, from more than one person except with the full knowledge of all interested parties.

DUTY OF PROFESSIONAL ENGINEER TO OTHER PROFESSIONAL ENGINEERS

4. A Professional Engineer shall,
   (a) not attempt to supplant another engineer after definite steps have been taken towards the other's employment;
   (b) not accept employment by a client, knowing that a claim for compensation or damages, or both, of a fellow engineer previously employed by the same client, and whose employment has been terminated, remains unsatisfied, or until such claim has been referred to arbitration or issue has been joined at law, or unless the engineer previously employed has neglected to press his claim legally, or the council of the Association gives its consent;
   (c) not accept any engagement to review the work of another professional engineer for the same employer except with the knowledge of that engineer, or except where the connection of that engineer with the work has been terminated;
   (d) not maliciously injure the reputation or business of another professional engineer;
   (e) not attempt to gain an advantage over other members of his profession by paying or accepting a commission in securing professional engineering work, or by reducing his fees below the approved minimums;
   (f) not advertise in a misleading manner or in a manner injurious to the dignity of his profession;
   (g) give proper credit for engineering work;
   (h) uphold the principle of adequate compensation for engineering work;
   (i) provide opportunity for professional development and advancement of his professional colleagues;

189

(j) extend the effectiveness of the profession through the interchange of engineering information and experiences.

DUTY OF PROFESSIONAL ENGINEER TO HIMSELF

5. A Professional Engineer shall,
   (a) maintain the honour and integrity of his profession and without fear or favour expose before the proper tribunals unprofessional or dishonest conduct by any other member of the profession;
   (b) undertake only such work as he is competent to perform by virtue of his training and experience; and
   (c) constantly strive to broaden his knowledge and experience by keeping abreast of new techniques and developments in his field of endeavour.

COMING INTO EFFECT

38. These Bylaws shall come into effect on the 30th day of November 1961.

Latest Revision Date Shown 1982.

THE ASSOCIATION OF PROFESSIONAL ENGINEERS OF THE YUKON TERRITORY

BY-LAWS

---

16. Code of Ethics
    (a) General

    A professional engineer owes certain duties to the public, to his employers, to his clients, to other members of his profession and to himself and shall act at all times with:

    1. fairness and loyalty to his associates, employers, clients, subordinates and employees;
    2. fidelity to public needs and
    3. devotion to high ideals of personal honour and professional integrity.

    (b) Duty of Professional Engineer to the Public

    A professional engineer shall:

    1. regard his duty to public welfare as paramount;
    2. endeavour at all times to enhance the public regard for his profession by extending the public knowledge thereof and discouraging untrue, unfair or exaggerated statements with respect to professional engineering;
    3. not give opinions or make statements, on professional engineering projects of public interest, that are inspired or paid for by private interests unless he clearly discloses on whose behalf he is giving the opinions or making the statements;
    4. not express publicly, or while he is serving as a witness before a court, commission or other tribunal, opinions on professional engineering matters that are not founded on adequate knowledge and honest conviction;
    5. make effective provisions for the safety of life and health of a person who may be affected by the work for which he is responsible; and at all times shall act to correct or report any situation which he feels may endanger the safety or welfare of the public;
    6. make effective provisions for meeting lawful standards, rules, or regulations relating to environmental control and protection in connection with any work being undertaken by him or under his responsibility;

191

7. sign or seal only those plans, specifications and reports made by him or under his personal supervision and direction or those which have been thoroughly reviewed by him as if they were his own work, and found to be satisfactory and

8. refrain from associating himself with or allowing the use of his name by an enterprise of questionable character.

(c) Duty of Professional Engineer to Employer

A professional engineer shall:

1. act in professional engineering matters for each employer as a faithful agent or trustee and shall regard as confidential any information obtained by him as to the business affairs, technical methods or processes of an employer and avoid or disclose any conflict of interest which might influence his actions or judgement;

2. present clearly to his employers the consequences to be expected from any deviations proposed in the work if he is informed that his professional engineering judgement is overruled by nontechnical authority in cases where he is responsible for the technical adequacy of professional engineering work;

3. have no interest, direct or indirect, in any materials, supplies or equipment used by his employer or in any persons or firms receiving contracts from his employer unless he informs his employer in advance of the nature of the interest;

4. not tender on competitive work upon which he may be acting as a professional engineer unless he first advises his employer;

5. not act as consulting engineer in respect of any work upon which he may be the contractor unless he first advises his employer, and

6. not accept compensation, financial or otherwise for a particular service from more than one person except with the full knowledge of all interested parties.

(d) Duty of Professional Engineer in Independent Practice to Client

A professional engineer in private practice, in addition to all other sections, shall:

1. disclose immediately any interest, direct or indirect, which may in any way be constituted as prejudicial to his professional judgement in rendering service to his client;

    2. if he is an employee-engineer and is contracting in his own name to perform professional engineering work for other than his employer, clearly advise his client as to the nature of his status as an employee and the attendant limitations on his services to the client. In addition he shall ensure that such work will not conflict with his duty to his employer;

    3. carry out his work in accordance with applicable statutes, regulations, standards, codes, and by-laws; and

    4. co-operate as necessary in working with such other professionals as may be engaged on a project.

(e) Duty of Professional Engineer to Other Professional Engineers

A professional engineer shall:

    1. conduct himself towards other professional engineers with courtesy and good faith;

    2. not accept any engagement to review the work of another professional engineer for the same employer or client except with the knowledge of that engineer, or except where the connection of that engineer with the work has been terminated;

    3. not maliciously injure the reputation or business of another professional engineer;

    4. not attempt to gain an advantage over other members of his profession by paying or accepting a commission in securing professional engineering work;

    5. not advertise in a misleading manner or in a manner injurious to the dignity of his profession, but shall seek to advertise by establishing a well-merited reputation for personal capability; and

    6. give proper credit for engineering work, uphold the principle of adequate compensation for engineering work, provide opportunity for professional development and advancement of his associates and subordinates; and extend the effectiveness of the profession through the interchange of engineering information and experience.

(f) Duty of Professional Engineer to Himself

A professional engineer shall:

    1. maintain the honour and integrity of his profession and without fear or favour expose before the proper tribunals unprofessional or dishonest conduct by any other members of the profession; and

    2. undertake only such work as he is competent to per-

form by virtue of his training and experience, and shall, where advisable, retain and co-operate with other professional engineers or specialists.

17. Repeal of Old By-Laws

Upon the coming into force of the foregoing By-Laws, all the By-Laws of the Association previously in force shall stand revoked.

Latest Revision Date Shown 1981.